NATURAL
BAKING

Carolin Strothe & Sebastian Keitel

NATURAL BAKING

Healthier recipes for a guilt-free treat

CONTENTS

CHOOSING THE RIGHT RECIPE

PREFACE

It's with great pleasure that I write the foreword for this beautiful book, created by one of Germany's very own superstar bakers, Carolin Strothe, and her creative genius of a husband, Sebastian Keitel.

I first met Carolin several years ago when she was one of the many food bloggers and vloggers I got to know on the culinary circuit. I have followed her work ever since on social media, and I can tell you that this chirpy, talented, passionate foodie is definitely the real deal. Carolin lives and breathes good food, and I mean in all areas of cooking, though of course she is particularly skilled in the baking department.

Carolin cherishes the seasonality of ingredients and keeping things natural, and she is a great advocate for local markets, farmers, and producers. In my opinion, she sums up the real fun and joy of contemporary German food.

You'll see from the pictures that her style is steeped in history, embracing the vibrancy and classic look of the Swing era, and that sense of heritage is also present in her food. On the one hand, the book is a sumptuous expression of proper German cooking, yet on the other an experimental, eccentric attitude comes through, and a wonderful curiosity for the rest of the world and its flavours.

This brilliant book is the culmination of the immense creative talent that Carolin and Sebastian share between them. Their joy for food, music, and dance, and their eye for design, photography, and colour just makes life that little bit brighter, and you'll experience that yourself as you flick through this book. Just like all of Carolin's recipes, when I see these gorgeous photographs, I want to tuck in immediately. I often want to eat my phone when she posts something new on Instagram (and if you're not already following her, what are you waiting for?!).

WHEN I LOOK AT THE GORGEOUS PHOTOS IN THIS BOOK, I WANT TO TUCK RIGHT IN.

The incredible bakes here are deliciously indulgent and tasty, but also designed to cut back on sugar. Baking is never going to be healthy, but Carolin strives to adopt a healthier approach in the creation of her recipes, and they don't disappoint. The celebration of ingredients and flavours is fantastic. I know this book will live happily in your home and be used often, and hopefully passed on to future generations. Enjoy it, and happy baking!

Jamie Oliver

INTRODUCTION

Why we are writing this book

We both associate childhood very strongly with special, carefree times spent outside in the garden. We enjoyed wonderful experiences, such as scoffing fruit from the berry bushes in summer and, in the autumn, gathering up old apple varieties, picking juicy pears, or collecting mushrooms in the woods. From an early age we learned from our parents and grandparents when each kind of fruit and vegetable was in season and how they could be used in cooking and baking. At the weekend a delicious cake would invariably be baked using freshly harvested fruit from the garden, so our intimate connection to nature began pretty much from birth. And nowadays we still love to unwind from the hustle and bustle of everyday life by baking timeless classic cakes at the weekend, or by giving them a new interpretation and enjoying the results with family and friends.

FROM EARLY ON WE LEARNED WHEN DIFFERENT FRUIT AND VEGETABLES WERE IN SEASON.

The health aspect of cooking also plays a big role in our recipes. As we grow older and our daily lives become more stressful, naturally we become more interested in our bodies and general health. This interest links to the topic of nutrition and its significant impact on our well-being. We have been focused on using natural ingredients in our food for over 15 years now, so eating healthily has become second nature and doesn't feel like an effort.

Once you begin to look more closely into nutrition, it soon becomes clear that the highly processed foods that are so ubiquitous are not only deficient in terms of natural ingredients, they also foster an unhealthy diet. Government research in 2017 found that almost 10 per cent of people in the UK rarely make food from scratch, and only 19 per cent cook from scratch each day. Shared meals are no longer an integral part of our daily routine as we eat at home far less often. Instead, people often grab food while they are on the move, eating when they happen to see something that looks delicious, or simply to fulfil a craving. In a dynamic world – where the key preoccupations are work, stress, or leisure activities – the motto is "quick and easy". Many kids no longer learn how to cook from scratch. In the past, girls were taught how to cook in domestic science lessons or grandmothers passed on their knowledge to the next generation. Today, too often this knowledge isn't passed on.

And yet the natural world continues to provide a diverse and rich cornucopia of ingredients that are incomparable when it comes to flavour. All too often ingredients are gradually being forgotten thanks to industrial-scale mass production. For understandable reasons, industrial production focuses on the ingredients that are easiest to use and which can be processed most efficiently to generate the largest revenues. High quantities of sugar and fat are often added to conceal the substandard quality of other ingredients. This situation is what prompted us to design and write this book. We want to restore our relationship with natural ingredients. Of course, there's an element of nostalgia involved, too, but, most importantly, it has become very clear that we are

harming ourselves and exploiting our planet with our current lifestyle, sometimes with disastrous and incalculable consequences. We would like our book to make a contribution (however small) to changing this.

Why we love sweet things

Have you ever tried to buy a tin of sour cherries without added sugar? It's really hard. Sugar is everywhere; concealed and unconcealed. It's a predicament: too much sugar is unhealthy, yet we love it. And no wonder, after all, we get our first taste of sugar from our mother's milk. Along with fat and protein, breast milk primarily contains the disaccharide lactose, which is what gives the milk its sweet taste. The reason we cannot resist sweet foods is due to a primal survival instinct. Sweet things are equated with goodness – we've sensed it in our bones from time immemorial. Our Stone Age ancestors were far more reliant on this sense of taste than we are today. Deciding whether to swallow something or spit it out was absolutely crucial to their survival. Their sense of taste functioned almost as a chemical sensor for the quality of different foods. Poisonous plants often taste bitter and acidic flavours can indicate that something

isn't ripe yet or that it is contaminated with bacteria. A "sweet" flavour, on the other hand, has positive associations. In particular, it serves as an indicator of high nutrient density. This was of immense importance to our prehistoric ancestors because they could never be sure when they would be getting their next meal or when they might experience a period of famine. So the human addiction to sugar is entirely natural from an evolutionary perspective and is the consequence of thousands of years of scarcity.

Apart from honey, food and drink with high levels of added sugar didn't appear in our diets until relatively recently. It was only when the industrial mass production of food took off that an excess of sweet dishes arose. A recent study found that many in the UK consume more than the daily recomended amount of sugar. This includes sugars added to food, as well as those that occur naturally, say, in honey and fruit juice. Experts all agree that too much sugar is being eaten. Poor diets combined with lack of exercise have seen a rise in so-called lifestyle conditions such as type 2 diabetes and obesity. As a result, in its new guidelines, the WHO (World Health Organization) has reduced the recommended daily intake of sugar to a maximum of 25g (scant 1oz).

If you read the ingredients lists on food packaging in more detail, you will quickly realize that it is almost impossible to buy packaged or processed foods or convenience goods without filling your shopping basket with additional sugar. Clearly it is crucial to regain control over our own sugar consumption and to handle sugar with more restraint. But how? The best way is to get into the kitchen and start cooking and baking yourself. That's the only way you can really control how much sugar, fat, and salt actually goes into your food. If you also use as many natural ingredients as possible, you will be well on the way to a healthy, pleasurable diet.

Sugar makes us happy because it triggers a response from the reward centre in our brain. On the other hand, sugar also makes you tired because there is an inevitable energy slump after the initial sugar high thanks to the way it causes our blood sugar levels to go up and down. The body then demands more sugar and so it goes on, and we end up consuming sugar without even noticing. Sugar is concealed in countless foods in the form of so-called empty carbohydrates, for example, in white flour. Often it is also combined with high quantities of saturated fats. One thing is absolutely clear: ultimately sugar is always sugar. It doesn't matter whether it is packaged as a soft drink, or as agave syrup, or whether you go back to natural sugars in the form of fruit (= fructose). Anything ending in "ose" contains sugar. So the solution is not just to use different sugars, but ideally also to use less.

The transition away from consuming high levels of refined sugar is a process that requires some adjustment. If you are used to eating lots of sugar, anything containing less sugar will initially taste strange. But by abstaining from refined sugars and products containing sugar for just 1–2 weeks, you will find your sensitivity to flavour increases very rapidly and you will be amazed just how sweet and "harsh" sugar tastes and how little of it you actually need. By following this approach, you will come to appreciate and recognize natural aromas and flavours. Sugars and sweeteners are not the only substances that taste sweet. For instance, cinnamon can also convey an impression of sweetness. And some natural ingredients, such as strawberries, taste inherently sweet. In fact, every variety of strawberry tastes fundamentally different.

MANY FRUIT VARIETIES TODAY ARE CULTIVATED SPECIFICALLY TO TASTE SWEETER.

Many fruit varieties today are cultivated specifically to taste sweeter. Apples, for instance, have been cultivated to remove polyphenols (see page 200). As a result, modern apple varieties taste sweet but are otherwise singularly lacking in flavour. Sweetness cannot be a substitute for flavour.

Nonetheless, enjoyable baking is impossible without sugar, so we don't renounce it completely. As advocates of diversity, we use different types of sugar from the classic, white processed variety. Sugars such as muscovado (whole cane sugar) do not taste as aggressively sweet and they have an interesting flavour of their own. Muscovado is less processed and still contains certain minerals. We also use as little sugar as possible for our recipes. As Paracelsus once said: "All things are poison and nothing is without poison; only the dose makes a thing not a poison."

Back to our roots

There are many arguments for using more wholesome and natural ingredients. In baking, not only will you benefit from high-quality nutrients and fibre, your cakes will also have far more exciting flavours and textures. White flour and sugar are rather lacking in flavour on their own. Wholemeal flours and ancient grain varieties, on the other hand, taste earthy, diverse, and nutty. Even smaller quantities can be enough to make you feel full and content.

Ancient grain varieties include heritage spelt, einkorn (see page 196), emmer (see page 197), rye and pseudo-grains such as buckwheat (see page 196) or teff (see page 198). Archaeological artefacts from around the time 10,000 BC prove that the cultivation of ancient grains has a long history. Einkorn and emmer, for instance, were first grown in the Middle East before spreading to Europe. Hildegard von Bingen (1098–1179) enthused about spelt in a number of different texts. And even at the start of the 19th century, spelt (see page 196) was the most widely cultivated grain in central Europe. However, wheat varieties with higher yields began to replace it and gradually took over more and more of the crop-growing areas until spelt fell almost completely into oblivion. Happily, it is currently experiencing something of a comeback, because spelt has excellent baking properties. We particularly like its nutty flavour and have been using it in many of our cakes and breads for over 15 years. Lots of alternative flour varieties are likewise enjoying a renaissance, such as almond flour (see page 197), cornmeal (see page 197) and chickpea, or gram, flour (see page 197). They taste naturally sweet, so your baking won't need as much additional sugar.

HAPPILY, ANCIENT GRAINS SUCH AS SPELT, EINKORN, AND EMMER ARE EXPERIENCING A COMEBACK.

Natural sweeteners have additional baking properties. Dates (see page 198), for example, are highly aromatic. Muscovado sugar (see page 199) has a strong flavour of its own, reminiscent of caramel, while maple syrup (see page 198) or apple purée (see page 192) will ensure your cakes are really moist.

Why we are passionate about natural ingredients

As consumers we have a choice about what we buy and eat. If we truly want a fair future for our grandchildren, we should inevitably be opting for organic, regional, and seasonal produce. Pesticide Action Network UK states that of the 490 pesticides approved by the EU, only 28 are approved for use in organic farming, all of which have low toxicity. On

the other hand, many of the pesticide substances used in conventional farming pose particular hazards for aquatic organisms, bees, other insects, and even for humans. Official figures have revealed that conventional fruit and vegetables have up to 200 times the quantities of pesticides as organic products. And the residues from these toxins are found everywhere – particularly in water. Organic farms, on the other hand, are permitted to use only limited agents to combat pests. One of the central components of organic farming is to use sophisticated crop rotation systems to minimize weeds and to keep the soil fertile. In addition, small biotopes – uniform environments – are deliberately created by organic farmers to provide valuable habitats for wild plants, soil organisms, and other animals.

The best approach of course is to use organic products that are both seasonal and regional. Remember that when you buy produce in its natural season from your regional area, you are not only supporting local farms and businesses, but also doing something good for the natural world. It's not surprising that consuming locally farmed lettuce, tomatoes, or apples grown between spring and

autumn (their natural growing season) achieves a better ecological balance than by importing fruit or vegetables from overseas during the same period.

Farmers who can sell their products at a local farmers' market don't need any intermediaries, which has many positive effects. The farmer can price goods more competitively, or at least consumers can be offered the price that would have been offered to the distributor. This in turn relieves the pressure to the farmer potentially caused by lower selling prices. The improved revenues from direct marketing can be invested by the farmer in better quality farming techniques and in the products themselves. If the farmer sells seasonal products, these will have been freshly harvested, and because they don't need to be transported far, they can be picked at the optimum harvesting time. So fruit and vegetables can be left to ripen fully and develop all their vitamins and nutrients quite naturally. When these products arrive freshly harvested at your table, they are higher in quality and have a better flavour.

When products go into storage, things are a bit different. If English apples are picked in October and stored in special conditions for several months, the energy consumption this requires can ultimately be higher than for imported apples. At around April, a point is reached where the energy balance tilts in favour of imported apples. But that doesn't change the fact that you can support local producers and thus retain more control over the food you buy. If you want to buy seasonal and regional fruit or vegetables, you should visit your local farmers' market or buy directly from the farmer. At farmers' markets, in particular, you will always find seasonal and regional products. In contrast to standard weekly markets, farmers' markets are always supplied by the producers themselves. If you are looking for exotic fruit, standard weekly markets usually supply these. Tropical fruit such as lemons and oranges provide variety in baking, especially in the winter months, and add a fresh note to a finished dish. For this reason,

we don't avoid these fruits completely, but overall we have tried to minimize the use of exotic ingredients in this book.

Generally, we favour baking with regional and seasonal ingredients. With many products – especially eggs and dairy produce – we advocate using organic products for animal welfare reasons (see page 196). You can also get seasonal and regional products from conventional farming, however, since the standard rules on pesticide use and animal welfare are generally so lax, we often find that there is no alternative to buying organic.

We are by no means preaching that you should avoid all luxury foods and sugar. And we are not trying to convert anyone to convert to veganism, vegetarianism, or an organic diet, nor do we advocate a paleo lifestyle or any other similar trend. We would just like to introduce you to baking with the most natural, original, and varied ingredients – exactly as they are found in nature. This also explains the title of our book: *Natural Baking*. This book should inspire you to explore the multitude of natural flavours in these foods and also to bake with more unusual ingredients, such as parsnips (see page 155) or kidney beans (see page 168). You will be amazed what delicious bakes you can conjure up!

Our recipes are marked with the following symbols to help you navigate the book:

gluten-free		preparation	
vegan		baking and cooking time	
lactose-free			
lactose-free option		resting time	
nut-free		chilling time	
no eggs			

THE SCENT
OF LILAC

We know that spring has finally arrived when green
shoots start to pop up and anemones and violets
blossom in the woods. With the long-awaited start
of spring, we bake with the first rhubarb, early
strawberries, and delicate edible flowers, while lilac
blooms emit their beguilingly delightful scent.

APPLE TART

Walnut Frangipane, Maple Syrup & Vanilla

Thanks to reliable natural storage methods, home-grown organic apples are available even in winter and spring, when they are still crisp and fresh, so our favourite fruit is always able to give this tart a harvest-fresh flavour. The crisp base is gluten-free, while the walnut cream rounds everything off perfectly.

☞ *MAKES 1 TART*

SHORTCRUST PASTRY

110g (3³/₄oz) jumbo oats (gluten-free)

15g (¹/₂oz) linseed

40g (1¹/₄oz) buckwheat flour

60g (2oz) cornflour

25g (scant 1oz) dark muscovado sugar

pinch of salt

120g (4¹/₄oz) chilled butter

60g (2oz) chilled buttermilk

FILLING

90g (3¹/₄oz) walnuts

1 tsp ground cinnamon

60ml (2fl oz) maple syrup, plus 1 tbsp for brushing

2 eggs

1–2 drops vanilla extract 600g (1lb 5oz) apples (4–5 apples)

2 tsp chilled butter

Blitz the oats in a food processor to create a flour and set aside 30g (1oz) of the oat flour for the filling. Finely crush the linseed using a pestle and mortar. Combine 80g (2³/₄oz) of oat flour with the linseed, buckwheat flour, cornflour, sugar, and salt in a bowl. Add the butter in little blobs and rub everything together with your fingers to form fine crumbs. Add the buttermilk and work swiftly to combine. Avoid handling the dough too much; it should remain fairly rough. Wrap in cling film and leave to rest for 20 minutes in the fridge.

To make the frangipane filling, grind the walnuts in a food processor to create a coarse flour. Place the remaining oat flour, cinnamon, maple syrup, eggs, and vanilla extract in a second bowl. Add the ground walnuts and stir until smoothly combined.

Preheat the oven to 180°C (350°F/Gas 4). Roll out the pastry on a sheet of baking parchment to create a large rectangle (roughly 28 × 30cm/11 x 12in) and place it on a baking tray. Spread the frangipane on top, leaving a 1cm (¹/₂in) border. Peel, quarter, and core the apples, then use a mandoline or knife to cut them into 3mm (¹/₈in) thin slices. Arrange little groups of five to six apple slices on the tart. Place the next group of slices at 90 degrees in a clockwise direction to the previous group and continue in this fashion to make an attractive pattern. Dot little blobs of butter over the top of the tart, fold up the edges, and press these in firmly.

Bake the tart in the centre of the oven for 30–35 minutes. Brush the hot tart with maple syrup.

🌾 | 🔨 *20 MINS* 🔲 *30 MINS* ❄ *30–35 MINS*

CARROT CAKE SWIRLS

Chickpea Flour, Vanilla & Almonds

These little cakes are such a simple affair. At first glance they seem unremarkable, but when eaten the combination of carrots and high-protein chickpea flour gives them a really special zing. The natural sweetness of the apple purée and maple syrup rounds off the flavour.

☞ *MAKES 12 SMALL CAKES (DIAMETER 5.5CM/2¼IN)*

CAKE MIXTURE

2 eggs

85ml (2¾fl oz) maple syrup

125ml (4¼fl oz) mild olive oil, plus extra for greasing

100g (3½oz) apple purée (see page 192)

1–2 drops vanilla extract

1 tsp ground cinnamon

120g (4¼oz) chickpea flour, plus extra for dusting

50g (1¾oz) ground almonds

50g (1¾oz) cornflour

2 tsp baking powder

pinch of salt

150ml (5fl oz) almond milk

150g (5½oz) carrots, peeled and roughly grated

ICING

1 quantity cashew icing (see page 193; optional)

DECORATION

Forget-me-not flowers (optional)

Preheat the oven to 180°C (350°F/Gas 4). Whisk the eggs and maple syrup for a few minutes in a bowl, gradually adding the oil. Stir in the apple purée, vanilla extract, and cinnamon.

In a second bowl, combine the chickpea flour, almonds, cornflour, baking powder, and salt. Add these dry ingredients to the egg mixture in stages, alternating with the milk. Mix everything gently, then fold the grated carrots into the cake mix.

Grease the moulds of a muffin tray or mini bundt pan with oil and dust with flour. Transfer the mixture into the moulds and bake for around 25 minutes, until risen and golden brown. When an inserted wooden skewer comes out clean, the little cakes are ready. Remove the cakes from the tin and leave to cool completely on a wire rack.

If icing the cakes, stir all the ingredients for the icing together. Cover the little cakes with the icing and, if using, decorate with forget-me-not blossom.

  | *20 MINS*  *25 MINS*

RHUBARB TARTLETS

Crispy Almond Shortcrust & Coconut Yogurt

Rhubarb is one of the first indigenous "vegetables" that we particularly look forward to baking with after the long winter. In this recipe we combine a perfectly balanced sweet and sour rhubarb-vanilla compote with coconut yogurt and almond shortcrust to conjure up spring on a plate.

 MAKES 8 TARTLETS (DIAMETER 10CM/4IN)

SHORTCRUST PASTRY

200g (7oz) spelt flour, plus extra for dusting

50g (1³/₄oz) ground almonds

20g (³/₄oz) dark muscovado sugar

½ tsp baking powder

pinch of salt

60ml (2fl oz) mild olive oil, plus extra for greasing

baking beans, for blind baking

FILLING AND TOPPING

300g (10oz) rhubarb, peeled and sliced into 3cm (1½in) pieces

grated zest of ½ organic orange

60ml (2fl oz) maple syrup

1 vanilla pod, halved lengthways and seeds removed

500g (1lb 2oz) coconut yogurt (see page 192)

Combine the flour, almonds, sugar, baking powder, and salt in a bowl. Add the oil and 60ml (2fl oz) water and work everything together quickly to form a dough. Avoid over-handling the dough; it should remain fairly rough. Shape into a ball, wrap in cling film, and leave to rest for 20 minutes in the fridge.

Meanwhile, bring the rhubarb, orange zest, maple syrup, and vanilla pod and seeds to the boil in 3½ tablespoons of water and simmer for 8–10 minutes, until soft. Leave the compote to cool.

Preheat the oven to 185°C (365°F/Gas 4½). Grease 8 tartlet tins and dust with flour. Divide the pastry into 8 equal portions and roll each one out into a circle on a floured work surface. Line the tartlet tins with the pastry, press the edges slightly, and trim off any overhanging pastry. Prick the pastry bases several times with a fork and chill for 15 minutes. Line the bases with pieces of baking parchment cut to size, weigh each piece down with baking beans, and blind bake the pastry for 17–20 minutes in the centre of the oven. Remove the baking beans and baking parchment, release the tartlets from their tins, and leave to cool. Fill with the coconut yogurt and top with the rhubarb compote.

Tip *Decorate with a piece of vanilla pod on top of each tart to make these rhubarb tartlets a bit more exotic.*

 | *35 MINS*  *30 MINS* ❄ *17-20 MINS*

Forget-me-not

Hollyhock

Lavender

Violets

Daisies

Gladioli

Elderflower

Sweet William

Horned violet

Rose

Dahlia

Blackberry
flower

Borage

Thyme

Phlox

Lilac

Camomile

Cosmos

Cornflower

Cherry blossom

Marigold

Apple Rose

French marigold

CARROT CAKE

Pumpkin Seeds, Apricots & Honey-Yogurt Icing

 MAKES 1 CAKE (DIAMETER 20CM/8IN)

CAKE MIXTURE

2 eggs

120ml (4fl oz) maple syrup

75ml (2¹/₂fl oz) mild vegetable oil, plus extra for greasing

¼ tsp black cardamom seeds

4 cloves

150g (5¹/₂oz) wholemeal spelt flour, plus extra for dusting

1 tsp ground cinnamon

pinch of grated nutmeg

2 tsp baking powder

pinch of salt

300g (10oz) carrots, peeled and finely grated

60g (2oz) dried apricots, chopped

grated zest of ½ organic orange

40g (1¹/₄oz) pumpkin seeds

ICING

150g (5¹/₂oz) full-fat cream cheese

150g (5¹/₂oz) yogurt of choice

25g (scant 1oz) acacia honey

2–3 drops vanilla extract

1 tbsp lemon juice

DECORATION

edible flowers and pumpkin seeds (optional)

Preheat the oven to 180°C (350°F/Gas 4). Beat the eggs and maple syrup in a bowl for several minutes with an electric whisk, gradually adding the oil. Finely grind the cardamom and cloves using a pestle and mortar. Combine the flour, spices, baking powder, and salt in a second bowl, add to the egg and oil mixture, and mix briefly. Fold the grated carrot, apricots, two-thirds of the orange zest, and the pumpkin seeds into the mixture.

Grease a springform tin (diameter 20cm/8in) with oil and dust with flour. Transfer the cake mix into the tin, smooth the surface, and bake in the centre of the oven for 35–40 minutes, until risen and golden brown. When an inserted wooden skewer comes out clean, the cake is ready. Carefully turn the warm cake out onto a wire rack and leave to cool completely.

For the icing, mix all the ingredients with most of the remaining orange zest and stir until smooth. Spread the mixture evenly over the cake. Sprinkle with the remaining orange zest and, if desired, decorate with edible flowers and some pumpkin seeds.

  25 MINS | 35–40 MINS

CHERRY BUNDT CAKE

Cocoa Nibs & Vanilla

This bundt cake can be made all year round using frozen sour cherries. The cocoa nibs are rich in magnesium and potassium and give the cake a strong chocolate flavour. In spring you can decorate it with cherry blossom in joyous anticipation of cherry season.

 MAKES 1 BUNDT CAKE (DIAMETER 14–16CM/5½–6¼IN)

CAKE MIXTURE

125g (4½oz) softened butter, plus extra for greasing

100g (3½oz) dark muscovado sugar

3 eggs

2–3 drops vanilla extract

200g (7oz) wholemeal spelt flour

50g (1¾oz) cornflour

3 tsp baking powder

pinch of salt

100ml (3½fl oz) milk of choice – we use almond milk

100g (3½oz) unsweetened sour cherries (canned or frozen)

30g (1oz) cocoa nibs

breadcrumbs for the tin

DECORATION

cherry and apple blossom (as desired)

Preheat the oven to 180°C (350°F/Gas 4). In a bowl, cream the butter and sugar for 3–5 minutes with an electric whisk. Stir in the eggs one at a time and add the vanilla extract. In a second bowl, combine the flour, cornflour, baking powder, and salt and stir the dry ingredients into the mixture a little at a time, stirring in some of the milk after each addition. Allow the thawed or preserved cherries to drain well then carefully fold into the cake mix with the cocoa nibs.

Grease a bundt tin with butter and sprinkle with breadcrumbs. Transfer the cake mix into the tin and bake in the centre of the oven for about 1 hour, until the cake has risen and is golden brown When an inserted wooden skewer comes out clean, the bundt cake is ready.

Leave to cool in the tin for about 10 minutes then turn out onto a wire rack to cool completely. If you wish, decorate with cherry and apple blossom.

Tip *Instead of cocoa nibs, you could also use chopped, high-quality dark chocolate with 70–85 per cent cocoa content.*

🔌 *20 MINS*   🍞 *1 HR*

CHERRY HOT CROSS BUNS

With Nutmeg, Cinnamon & Vanilla

These traditional Good Friday buns, which get their name from the characteristic cross made using a flour paste, are an extremely popular Easter treat. The secret ingredient in this particular recipe comes in the form of pre-soaked dried sour cherries.

☞ *MAKES 12 BUNS*

YEAST DOUGH

250ml (9fl oz) milk of choice
  – we use almond milk

60g (2oz) dark muscovado sugar

10g (¹/₄oz) dried yeast

2–3 drops vanilla extract

1 tsp ground cinnamon

pinch of grated nutmeg

pinch of salt

450g (1lb) spelt flour, plus extra
  for dusting

60g (2oz) softened butter

1 egg

80g (2³/₄oz) dried sour cherries
  (or cranberries or raisins)

100ml (3¹/₂fl oz) orange juice

TOPPING

40g (1¹/₄oz) spelt flour

3 tbsp apricot jam (70 per cent
  fruit content)

To make the yeast dough, heat the milk in a pan until lukewarm. Add the sugar, yeast, vanilla extract, cinnamon, nutmeg, and salt and stir well until the yeast has completely dissolved. Use the dough hook attachment on an electric mixer to combine the flour with the yeast mixture, butter, and egg for a couple of minutes in a bowl until you have a glossy and supple dough. The dough will be very soft and silky – exactly how it should be. Cover with a tea towel and leave to prove in a warm place for about 1 hour, until doubled in size. Meanwhile, soak the sour cherries in the orange juice. After about 1 hour, pour off the juice and leave to drain well.

Knead the dough thoroughly on a floured work surface and carefully work the sour cherries into the dough. Divide into 12 equal portions and shape into round buns. Place the buns, spaced a little apart, on two baking trays lined with baking paper. Cover with tea towels and leave to prove in a warm place for a further 30 minutes.

To make the crosses, stir the flour into 2 tablespoons of water to form a smooth paste, transfer to a piping bag with a medium nozzle, and carefully pipe crosses onto the buns.

Preheat the oven to 185°C (365°F/Gas 4¹/₂). Bake the hot cross buns in the centre of the oven for about 16–19 minutes per tray, until golden brown, then transfer to a wire rack and glaze with apricot jam while they are still hot. Serve while still warm; the buns go perfectly with some butter and jam.

 | 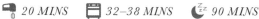 20 MINS   32–38 MINS Zᶻ 90 MINS

DOUBLE CHOCOLATE MUFFINS

With Avocado Chocolate Mousse

These moist vegan chocolate muffins are given a special twist thanks to the espresso. The plant-based icing made from banana, avocado, and cocoa is a splendid addition and a healthier option than buttercream icing, while the violets add a sensual touch with their tantalizing scent.

☞ *MAKES 12 MUFFINS*

MUFFIN MIXTURE

2 tsp cider vinegar

200ml (7fl oz) almond milk

2–3 drops vanilla extract

60g (2oz) mild coconut oil

320g (11oz) spelt flour

160g (5³⁄₄oz) dark
   muscovado sugar

6 tbsp cocoa powder

4 tsp baking powder

pinch of salt

3¹⁄₂ tbsp cold espresso

FROSTING

2 ripe avocados

2 ripe bananas

3 tbsp maple syrup

4 tbsp mild coconut oil

8 tsp cocoa powder

2–3 drops vanilla extract

DECORATION

24 violet flowers (optional)

Preheat the oven to 180°C (350°C/Gas 4). Whisk the cider vinegar, almond milk, and vanilla extract together in a bowl and set aside. Melt the coconut oil in a pan over a low heat. Combine the flour, sugar, cocoa powder, baking powder, and salt in a large bowl. Add the almond milk mixture, coconut oil, and espresso and stir briefly until combined.

Fill the moulds of a muffin tray with 12 paper cases. Divide the mixture evenly between the cases and bake in the centre of the oven for 18–22 minutes, until risen. When an inserted wooden skewer comes out clean, the muffins are ready. Remove from the tray and leave to cool on a wire rack.

To make the frosting, purée the avocado flesh, bananas, and remaining ingredients until the icing is glossy and silky-smooth. Chill in the fridge for 30 minutes then decant into a piping bag with a flower nozzle and pipe onto the muffins. If you wish, decorate with some violets.

  20 MINS  *18–22 MINS* ❄ *30 MINS*

COURGETTE CAKE

Elderflower, Pistachio & Yogurt Icing

 MAKES 1 CAKE
(11 × 25CM/
4½ X 10IN)

CAKE MIXTURE

125g (4½oz) softened butter,
    plus extra for greasing

160g (5¾oz) dark
    muscovado sugar

3 eggs

2–3 drops vanilla extract

juice and grated zest of
    ½ organic lemon

100g (3½oz) pistachios

150g (5½oz) spelt flour, plus
    extra for dusting

100g (3½oz) wholemeal spelt

5 tsp baking powder

6 elderflower heads

400g (14oz) courgette,
    finely grated

pinch of salt

ICING

1 tsp cornflour

1tsp icing sugar

120g (4½oz) Greek yogurt

2 tbsp acacia honey

2 tsp lemon juice

DECORATION

2–3 elderflower heads

grated zest of ½ organic lemon

2 tbsp pistachios

1 tbsp pumpkin seeds

Preheat the oven to 180°C (350°F/Gas 4). Cream the butter and sugar in a bowl for 3–5 minutes, until light and fluffy. Stir in the eggs one at a time. Add the vanilla extract and the lemon juice and zest and mix. Finely grind the pistachios in a food processor or grinder. Combine the pistachios, both types of flour, and the baking powder, add to the mix, and stir briefly. Shake the elderflower heads and strip off the flowers. Fold the courgette, salt, and elderflowers into the cake mix.

Grease a loaf tin (11 × 25cm/4½ x 10in) with butter and dust with flour. Transfer the cake mix into the tin and bake in the centre of the oven for 35–40 minutes, until risen and golden brown. When an inserted wooden skewer comes out clean, the cake is ready. Leave to cool in the tin for about 10 minutes, then turn out onto a wire rack and leave to cool completely.

For the icing, stir the cornflour and icing sugar into the yogurt, then add the honey and lemon juice and combine until smooth. Spread the mixture evenly over the cake. Shake the elderflower heads and strip off the flowers. Decorate the cake with elderflowers, lemon zest, pistachios, and pumpkin seeds.

Tip *This cake still tastes fantastic without the flowers outside of elderflower season. For a variation, instead of using ground pistachios you can try ground almonds or hazelnuts.*

25 MINS   *35–40 MINS*

STRAWBERRY
AND ALMOND MUFFINS

Almond Flour & Elderflowers

Spring meets summer in this recipe. The fragrant elderflowers give these muffins a unique flavour, and the combination of ripe strawberries with the delicate blossom creates a real explosion of flavours. The gluten- and lactose-free almond flour helps to keep the muffins moist.

 MAKES 10 MUFFINS

MUFFIN MIXTURE

3 eggs

60g (2oz) dark muscovado sugar

2–3 drops vanilla extract

3½ tbsp mild vegetable oil

200g (7oz) buttermilk

150g (5½oz) almond flour

2 tsp baking powder

pinch of salt

3 elderflower heads

100g (3½oz) strawberries, hulled and chopped into small pieces

DECORATION

elderflowers and strawberry halves (as desired)

Preheat the oven to 180°C (350°F/Gas 4). Beat the eggs, sugar, and vanilla extract in a bowl for several minutes with an electric whisk until the mixture is pale. Add the oil and buttermilk. In a second bowl, combine the almond flour, baking powder, and salt. Add the dry ingredients in batches to the egg and buttermilk mixture.

Shake the elderflowers and strip off the flowers. Carefully fold the elderflowers and strawberry pieces into the muffin mixture. Fill the moulds of a muffin tray with 10 paper cases. Divide the mixture evenly between the cases and bake the muffins in the centre of the oven for 18–22 minutes, until risen and golden brown. When an inserted wooden skewer comes out clean, they are ready. Leave the muffins to cool on a wire rack. If you wish, decorate with the elderflowers and strawberries.

Tip Outside elderflower season, you can omit the flowers and just bake the muffins with strawberries.

 | *15 MINS* *18–22 MINS*

PEANUT BLONDIES

Chickpeas, Vanilla & Dark Chocolate

Blondies are the pale sister to brownies. Our version is packed with peanut power, chickpea protein bombs, and dark chocolate, a superb flavour combination that is bound to boost your spirits. Moreover, if you make these in the food processor, they are very quick to prepare.

 MAKES 9 BLONDIES

BLONDIE MIX

215g (7¹/₂oz) chickpeas (from a jar, drained weight)

60g (2oz) unsalted peanut butter

60g (2oz) cashew nut butter

100ml (3¹/₂fl oz) maple syrup

2–3 drops vanilla extract

½ tsp baking powder

50g (1³/₄oz) dark chocolate, 70 per cent cocoa content, chopped

coconut oil for greasing and teff flour or cornflour for dusting

DECORATION

dark chocolate, 70 per cent cocoa content, chopped (optional)

Preheat the oven to 180°C (350°F/Gas 4). Drain the chickpeas and wash thoroughly in cold water. Purée all the ingredients except the chocolate in a food processor until smooth, then add the chocolate and fold into the mix.

Grease a square baking tin (20–21cm/8–8¹/₄in) with coconut oil and dust with flour or cornflour. Transfer the blondie mixture into the tin, smooth the surface, and bake for about 25 minutes in the centre of the oven, until pale golden in colour. Leave to cool completely on a wire rack before cutting into pieces. If you wish, decorate with some chocolate pieces.

Tip   *To make a vegan version you could use vegan dark chocolate. If tightly sealed and stored in the fridge, the blondies will keep for 4–5 days.*

 10 MINS   *25 MINS*

BUILDING BLOCKS: OAT MUFFINS

One Mix – Six Options

 MAKES 12 MUFFINS

① THE BASIC MIX

300g (10oz) jumbo oats (gluten-free)
1 tsp ground cinnamon
1 tsp baking powder
pinch of salt
400ml (14fl oz) almond milk
2–3 drops vanilla extract
125ml ($4^{1}/_{4}$fl oz) maple syrup
oil and cornflour for greasing and dusting

Combine the ingredients in a large bowl until well mixed. Leave to swell for about 10 minutes. Preheat the oven to 185°C (365°F/Gas $4^{1}/_{2}$). Grease the moulds of a muffin tray and dust with flour.

② BLUEBERRY AND ALMOND

150g ($5^{1}/_{2}$oz) blueberries
70g ($2^{1}/_{4}$oz) almonds, chopped

or

PEANUT BUTTER AND BANANA

280g ($9^{1}/_{2}$oz) bananas (about 2 bananas),
peeled and mashed
125g ($4^{1}/_{2}$oz) unsalted peanut butter

or

RASPBERRY AND CASHEW

150g ($5^{1}/_{2}$oz) raspberries
70g ($2^{1}/_{4}$oz) cashew nuts, chopped

or

APPLE AND CINNAMON

150g ($5^{1}/_{2}$oz) apple, chopped (about 2 apples)
1 tsp ground cinnamon

or

CRANBERRY AND WALNUT

150g ($5^{1}/_{2}$oz) dried cranberries
grated zest of ½ organic orange
70g ($2^{1}/_{4}$oz) walnuts, chopped

or

CARROT AND TURMERIC

70g ($2^{1}/_{4}$oz) carrot, finely grated
pinch of grated nutmeg
pinch of ground cloves
50g ($1^{3}/_{4}$oz) dried apricots, chopped
1 tsp grated turmeric

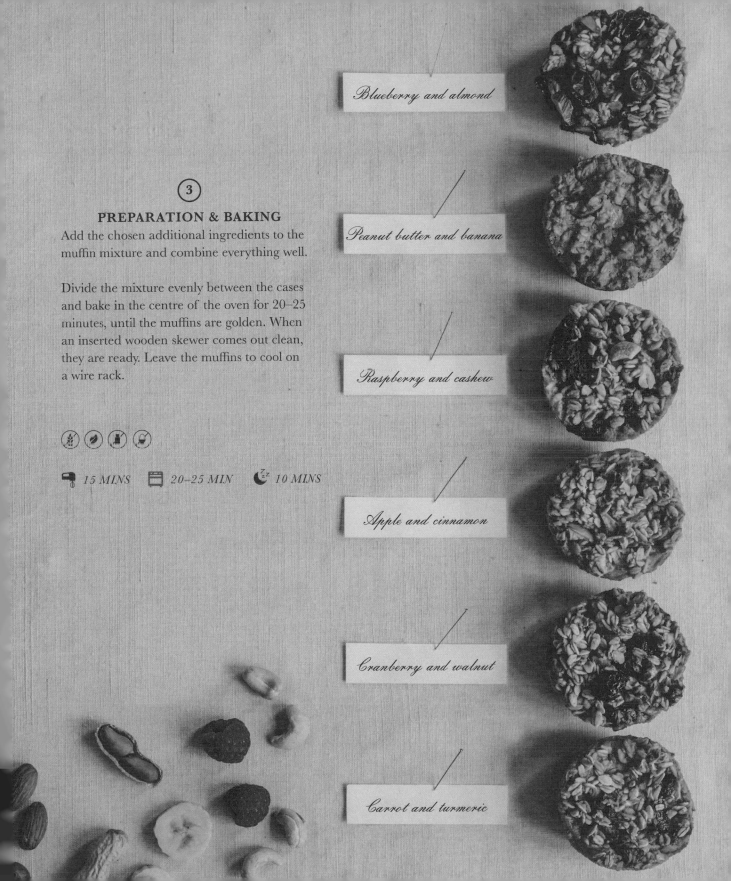

③

PREPARATION & BAKING

Add the chosen additional ingredients to the muffin mixture and combine everything well.

Divide the mixture evenly between the cases and bake in the centre of the oven for 20–25 minutes, until the muffins are golden. When an inserted wooden skewer comes out clean, they are ready. Leave the muffins to cool on a wire rack.

15 MINS   *20–25 MIN*   *10 MINS*

Blueberry and almond

Peanut butter and banana

Raspberry and cashew

Apple and cinnamon

Cranberry and walnut

Carrot and turmeric

TEFF WAFFLES

Elderflower & Vanilla

When the first elderflower bushes begin to blossom in spring, we always make sure we take a basket and scissors on cycling excursions (see tip, below) because the window for harvesting these delicate, aromatic flowers is so brief. The white flower heads can be used for all sorts of recipes, both sweet and savoury.

 MAKES ABOUT 8 WAFFLES (8.5 × 14CM/ 3½ X 5½IN)

BATTER

250ml (9fl oz) milk of choice
 – we use almond milk

4g dried yeast

60g (2oz) dark muscovado sugar

2 eggs

300g (10oz) teff flour

100g (3½oz) cornflour

2 tsp baking powder

2–3 drops vanilla extract

125ml (4¼fl oz) mild vegetable
 oil, plus extra for greasing

pinch of salt

6–8 elderflower heads

Heat the milk and 200ml (7fl oz) water in a pan until lukewarm then remove from the hob. Dissolve the yeast and sugar in the lukewarm liquid.

Separate the eggs. In a bowl, combine the flour, cornflour, and the baking powder. Add the milk mixture, egg yolks, and vanilla extract and stir until you have a smooth batter. Add the oil and stir it in. In a separate bowl, whisk the egg whites with the salt until stiff and carefully fold into the waffle mixture using a balloon whisk. Cover with a tea towel and leave to stand in a warm place for 20 minutes.

Shake the elderflowers and strip off the flowers. Oil and preheat the waffle iron. For each waffle, put 2 tablespoons of the mix onto the iron, scatter with elderflowers, and cook until golden. Continue in this way until all the batter has been used. If you wish, serve the waffles with rhubarb compote (see page 22) and scatter raspberries on top.

Tip *It is best to pick elderflowers on a dry, sunny morning. Only then will the elderflowers be in full bloom and have their intense aroma. Always pick the flowers in open countryside to avoid potential pollution from traffic. The flowers wilt quickly, so you need to use them swiftly. Don't rinse them because this will wash off the pollen, which provides the flavour. Once elderflower season is over, the waffles will still taste fantastic without their addition. You can vary this recipe by folding 50g (1¾oz) of chopped almonds into the mix.*

  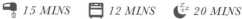 *15 MINS* | *12 MINS* | *20 MINS*

BERRY ICE-CREAM CAKE

Muesli Base & Berry Layers

*This "nice-cream" tart is ideal for hot days and offers a splendid alternative to heavy cream cakes.
You won't need an oven for this recipe because this raw cake simply consists of a muesli base with berry
ice-cream layers. In early summer, you can decorate the cake with sweet lilac blossom.*

☞ **MAKES 1 CAKE
(DIAMETER
20CM/8IN)**

BASE

80g (2³/₄oz) desiccated coconut

100g (3¹/₂oz) almonds

50g (1³/₄oz) mild coconut oil

75g (2¹/₂oz) dates

2–3 drops vanilla extract

ICE-CREAM LAYERS

200g (7oz) frozen blueberries

3 large bananas, about
450g/1lb

6 drops vanilla extract

200g (7oz) frozen blackberries

200g (7oz) frozen raspberries

DECORATION

150g (5¹/₂oz) mixed
frozen berries

lilac blossom (optional)

Put all the ingredients for the base into a food processor and blitz until smooth. Transfer the mixture to a springform tin (diameter 20cm/8in) and press down to form an even base.

To make the blueberry layer, blitz the frozen blueberries, 1 banana (150g/5¹/₂oz), and 2 drops of the vanilla extract in a food processor until you have a creamy ice mixture. Spread this over the muesli base and smooth the surface. Transfer to the freezer for 1–2 hours until set.

To make the blackberry layer, blitz the frozen blackberries, 1 banana (150g/5¹/₂oz) and 2 drops of the vanilla extract in the food processor. Spread this mixture over the first layer and smooth the surface. Return to the freezer for another 1–2 hours, until the mixture has set.

To make the raspberry layer, blitz the frozen raspberries, the remaining banana, and the rest of the vanilla extract in the food processor. Spread this mixture over the second layer and smooth the surface. Return to the freezer for a final 1–2 hours, until this top layer has set.

Let the cake defrost for 30–45 minutes before serving and decorate with frozen berries and lilac blossom, as desired.

   30 MINS ❄ *3–6 HRS*  *30–45 MINS*

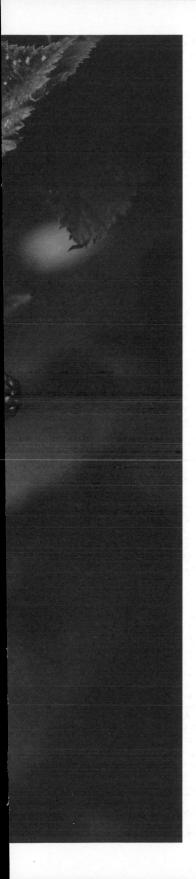

FROM THE
ORCHARD

The arrival of summer heralds the most perfect
culinary paradise. Ripened sun-kissed berries hang
from bushes, bringing joy to your plate, and you can
make the most of the short season for stoned fruit by
indulging in exquisite cakes under clear blue skies.

REDCURRANT TEFF COOKIES

Hazelnuts & Dates

These redcurrant cookies are perfect for a quick break with a cup of tea. The gluten-free teff flour is rich in essential fatty acids, potassium, and phosphorous. Here, the flour combines beautifully with the redcurrants, dates, and hazelnuts to create a handy energy-boosting snack.

☞ *MAKES 12 COOKIES*

COOKIE DOUGH

90g (3^{1}/$_{4}$oz) hazelnuts

100g (3^{1}/$_{2}$oz) dried dates,
   finely chopped

90g (3^{1}/$_{4}$oz) teff flour

50g (1^{3}/$_{4}$oz) cornflour

½ tsp baking powder

pinch of salt

110g (3^{3}/$_{4}$oz) chilled butter

1 egg

2–3 drops vanilla extract

100g (3^{1}/$_{2}$oz) redcurrants

90g (3^{1}/$_{4}$oz) jumbo oats
   (gluten-free)

Toast the hazelnuts in a dry pan over a moderate heat until pale brown and fragrant. Set aside and leave to cool. Place the dates in a saucepan with 2 tablespoons of water and bring to the boil, then simmer gently until soft. Purée and leave to cool.

Combine the teff flour, cornflour, baking powder, and salt in a bowl. Add the butter in little blobs and rub everything together with your fingers to form fine crumbs. Add the date purée, egg, and vanilla extract and work everything swiftly until combined. Avoid overhandling the dough; the texture should remain fairly rough. Roughly chop the hazelnuts. Carefully work the redcurrants, oats, and hazelnuts into the cookie dough, trying not to squash the berries too much. Leave the dough to rest in the fridge for 30 minutes.

Preheat the oven to 180°C (350°F/Gas 4). Shape the cookie dough into 12 equal-sized balls. Place the balls some distance apart on two baking trays lined with baking parchment and press them to flatten them slightly. Baking one tray at a time, bake the cookies in the centre of the oven for 12–15 minutes, until golden brown. Leave to cool – these very crumbly cookies become firmer as they cool. The cookies taste best fresh, but can also be stored in an airtight container in a cool place for 2–3 days.

Tip   *Instead of using fresh redcurrants, these cookies can also be made with 75g (2^{1}/$_{2}$oz) dried fruit such as raisins, sour cherries, or cranberries. Soak the dried fruit beforehand in 75ml (2½fl oz) orange juice for 1–2 hours, then drain well before mixing into the cookie dough.*

 | 🥄 *20 MINS*   🍞 *24–30 MINS*   ❄ *30 MINS*

SPRING TRAY BAKE

Raspberries, Fresh Currants, Strawberries & Rhubarb

There is something here for everyone: tart rhubarb, sweet strawberries, the season's first raspberries, and fresh currants. Early summer offers only a brief window of opportunity for this exquisite combination of ingredients. This tray bake is easy and quick to make, and the ingredients can be changed as you wish.

☞ *MAKES 1 TRAY BAKE*

CAKE MIX

250g (9oz) softened butter

150g (5^1/$_2$oz) acacia honey

5 eggs

1–2 drops vanilla extract

grated zest of 1 organic lemon

250g (9oz) spelt flour

100g (3^1/$_2$oz) ground almonds

5 tsp baking powder

pinch of salt

100ml (3^1/$_2$fl oz) milk of choice
 – we use almond milk

FILLING

225g (8oz) raspberries

200g (7oz) strawberries, halved
 and hulled

175g (6oz) fresh currants (white,
 red, or black), stalks removed

4 sticks of rhubarb
 (30cm/12in long)

1 tbsp dark muscovado sugar

Preheat the oven to 180°C (350°F/Gas 4). Cream the butter and honey in a bowl for 3–5 minutes. Stir in the eggs one at a time. Add the vanilla extract and lemon zest. In a second bowl, combine the flour, almonds, baking powder, and salt. Add the dry ingredients in batches to the butter mixture, alternating with the milk and mixing briefly.

Spread the mixture over a baking tray lined with baking parchment. Arrange the raspberries, strawberries, currants, and rhubarb on separate quarters of the cake and sprinkle evenly with the sugar. Bake the cake in the centre of the oven for 30–35 minutes, until risen and golden brown. When an inserted wooden skewer comes out clean, the cake is ready. Remove from the oven and leave to cool.

25 MINS   *30–35 MINS*

STRAWBERRY AND ALMOND CAKE

Almond Sponge & Vanilla Cream

This cake has so many happy associations for us – from picking strawberries in our own garden to bicycle excursions to the pick-your-own farm. The light almond sponge is quick to make and is topped with a fromage frais cream and plenty of fresh berries.

☞ *MAKES 1 CAKE (DIAMETER 26CM / 10½IN)*

SPONGE

3 eggs

70g (2½oz) dark muscovado sugar

pinch of salt

80g (2¾oz) ground almonds

40g (1¼oz) cornflour, plus extra for dusting

1 tsp baking powder

butter for greasing

TOPPING

250g (9oz) low-fat quark

1 tbsp maple syrup or honey

1–2 drops vanilla extract

300g (10oz) strawberries, halved

150g (5½oz) redcurrants or extra strawberries

daisies, to decorate (optional)

Preheat the oven to 190°C (375°F/Gas 5). Separate the eggs. In a bowl, beat the egg yolks with 40g (1¼oz) of the sugar and 6 tablespoons of water using an electric whisk until thick and foamy. Whisk the egg whites separately with the salt until stiff, trickling in the remaining sugar as you go. Combine the almonds, cornflour, and baking powder. Carefully fold the whisked egg whites into the egg yolk mixture. Sift over the almond mixture and fold in swiftly with a balloon whisk.

Grease a springform tin (diameter 26cm/10½in) with butter and dust with cornflour. Transfer the cake mix into the tin, smooth the surface, and bake in the centre of the oven for 18–22 minutes, until risen and golden brown. When an inserted wooden skewer comes out clean, the cake is ready. Release from the tin and leave to cool on a wire rack.

To make the cream topping, stir the fromage frais, maple syrup or honey, and vanilla extract together until smooth and spread evenly over the cake base. Scatter the fruit over the cake and, if you wish, decorate with daisies. Chill in the fridge for 30 minutes before serving.

 | 🔌 *15 MINS*   🔲 *18–22 MINS*   ❄ *30 MINS*

VICTORIA SPONGE CAKE

Raspberries & Rose Petals

In summer we love indulging in leisurely picnics in the garden, and these occasions are never without a Victoria sponge, a classic component of afternoon tea. Our version uses spelt, raspberries, and rose water.

☞ *MAKES 1 CAKE (DIAMETER 20CM/8IN)*

CAKE MIX

150g (5¹/₂oz) softened butter, plus extra for greasing

80g (2³/₄oz) dark muscovado sugar

2–3 drops vanilla extract

3 eggs

grated zest of ½ organic orange

3¹/₂ tbsp milk

150g (5¹/₂oz) wholemeal spelt flour, plus extra for dusting

2 tsp baking powder

pinch of salt

FILLING

75g (2¹/₂oz) raspberries (fresh or frozen), plus raspberry jam

1 tsp dark muscovado sugar

20 drops rose water

100g (3¹/₂oz) whipping cream

2–3 drops vanilla extract

1 tsp cornflour

1tsp icing sugar

100g (3¹/₂oz) Greek yogurt

150g (5¹/₂oz) raspberries

DECORATION

100g (3¹/₂oz) raspberries

rose petals

Preheat the oven to 180°C (350°F/Gas 4). Cream the butter, sugar, and vanilla in a bowl for a few minutes using an electric whisk until the mixture is pale. Stir in the eggs one at a time. Add the orange zest and milk. In a second bowl, combine the flour, baking powder, and salt and add this in batches to the butter and egg mixture, stirring only briefly. Grease two springform tins (diameter 20cm/8in) with butter and dust with the flour. Divide the cake mix equally between the tins, smooth the surface, and bake in the centre of the oven for 18–20 minutes, until the cakes have risen and are golden brown in colour. When an inserted wooden skewer comes out clean, they are ready. Release from the tins and leave to cool on a wire rack for at least 30 minutes.

For the filling, bring the raspberries and sugar to the boil in a pan. Lower the heat and simmer for a couple of minutes, stirring occasionally until the liquid has reduced and resembles a thick jam in consistency. Leave the jam to cool then stir in the rose water.

Whip the cream, vanilla extract, cornflour, and icing sugar until stiff, then fold in the yogurt. Place one of the cake halves on a cake platter and spread with jam. Cover with the whipped cream filling and most of the fresh raspberries. Place the second cake half on top. Decorate the cake with the extra raspberries and the rose petals. Chill in the fridge for 30–60 minutes before serving.

Tip *You could also try making this cake with strawberries.*

 | 🔌 *20 MINS* 📟 *18–20 MINS* ❄ *30–60 MINS* 💤 *30 MINS* ____

APPLE WAFFLES

One Waffle – Lots of Toppings

Apple waffles with mineral-rich spelt flour are really easy to make and they are a great alternative to traditional waffle recipes. Our version is vegan and you can let your imagination run wild when it comes to the toppings. It won't be long before everyone in the family has decided on their favourite combo!

 MAKES 10 HEART-SHAPED WAFFLES

BATTER

600ml (1 pint) plant-based milk – we use almond milk

10g (¹/₄oz) dried yeast

100ml (3¹/₂fl oz) maple syrup

500g (1lb 2oz) spelt flour

2 tsp ground cinnamon

pinch of salt

150ml (5fl oz) mild vegetable oil, plus extra for greasing

400g (14oz) apples (about 3 apples), peeled and roughly grated

toppings of choice, to serve (see tip, opposite)

Heat the milk in a pan until lukewarm, then remove from the hob. Dissolve the yeast and maple syrup in the warmed milk. Combine the flour, cinnamon, and salt in a bowl. Add the milk mixture and the oil and whisk briefly using an electric whisk until you have a smooth batter. Cover with a tea towel and leave to prove in a warm place for 30 minutes to 1 hour.

Fold the grated apples into the batter. Oil and preheat the waffle iron. For each waffle, put 2 tablespoons of the mixture onto the iron and cook until golden. Continue in this way until all the batter has been used. Serve with fresh fruit, yogurt, or other toppings of your choice (see tip, below).

Tip   *Add one or more of the following toppings: blueberries; blackberries; fresh currants; raspberries; strawberries; apple; pear; damson; grapes; banana; frozen berries; (coconut) yogurt; fruit yogurt; fruit powder; maple syrup; honey; jam (70 per cent fruit content); coulis made from frozen raspberries; almonds; cashew nuts; hazelnuts; walnuts; pumpkin seeds; poppy seeds; popcorn; dark chocolate; cocoa nibs; coconut chips; nut butters (such as peanut); apple purée; edible flowers; mint, and so on.*

  15 MINS *30 MINS*  *30–60 MINS*

YOGURT CAKE

Einkorn, Gooseberries & Redcurrants

The yogurt in this recipe gives this cake a fresh, light texture and also adds moisture, while the protein-rich einkorn flour ensures a wonderful crispness. Combined with gooseberries and redcurrants, the result is a sweet and sour tang that really is addictive.

 MAKES 1 CAKE (DIAMETER 20CM/8IN)

CAKE MIX

2 eggs

125g (4¹/₂oz) dark muscovado sugar

2–3 drops vanilla extract

125ml (4¹/₄fl oz) mild olive oil, plus extra for greasing

250g (9oz) yogurt of choice

250g (9oz) einkorn (or wholemeal spelt flour), plus extra for dusting

5 tsp baking powder

pinch of salt

150g (5¹/₂oz) gooseberries, stalks removed

150g (5¹/₂oz) fresh redcurrants

DECORATION

fresh redcurrants and gooseberries

dahlia flower petals (optional)

Preheat the oven to 180°C (350°F/Gas 4). In a bowl, cream the eggs, sugar, and vanilla extract with an electric whisk for a few minutes until the mixture is pale. Add the olive oil and yogurt and stir together. In a second bowl, combine the einkorn, baking powder, and salt and add this in batches to the egg and yogurt mixture. Stir briefly – just long enough to combine everything. Carefully fold the gooseberries and redcurrants into the cake mix.

Grease a springform tin (diameter 20cm/8in) and dust with some of the flour. Transfer the cake mix into the tin, smooth the surface, and bake in the centre of the oven for 35–40 minutes, until risen and golden brown. When an inserted wooden skewer comes out clean, the cake is ready. Release from the tin and leave to cool on a wire rack. For the decoration, arrange the berries together with the flower petals, if using, on the cake.

Tip   *Instead of gooseberries and redcurrants, berries such as raspberries and blackberries or fruit such as apricots and sour cherries also work well here.*

20 MINS   35–40 MINS

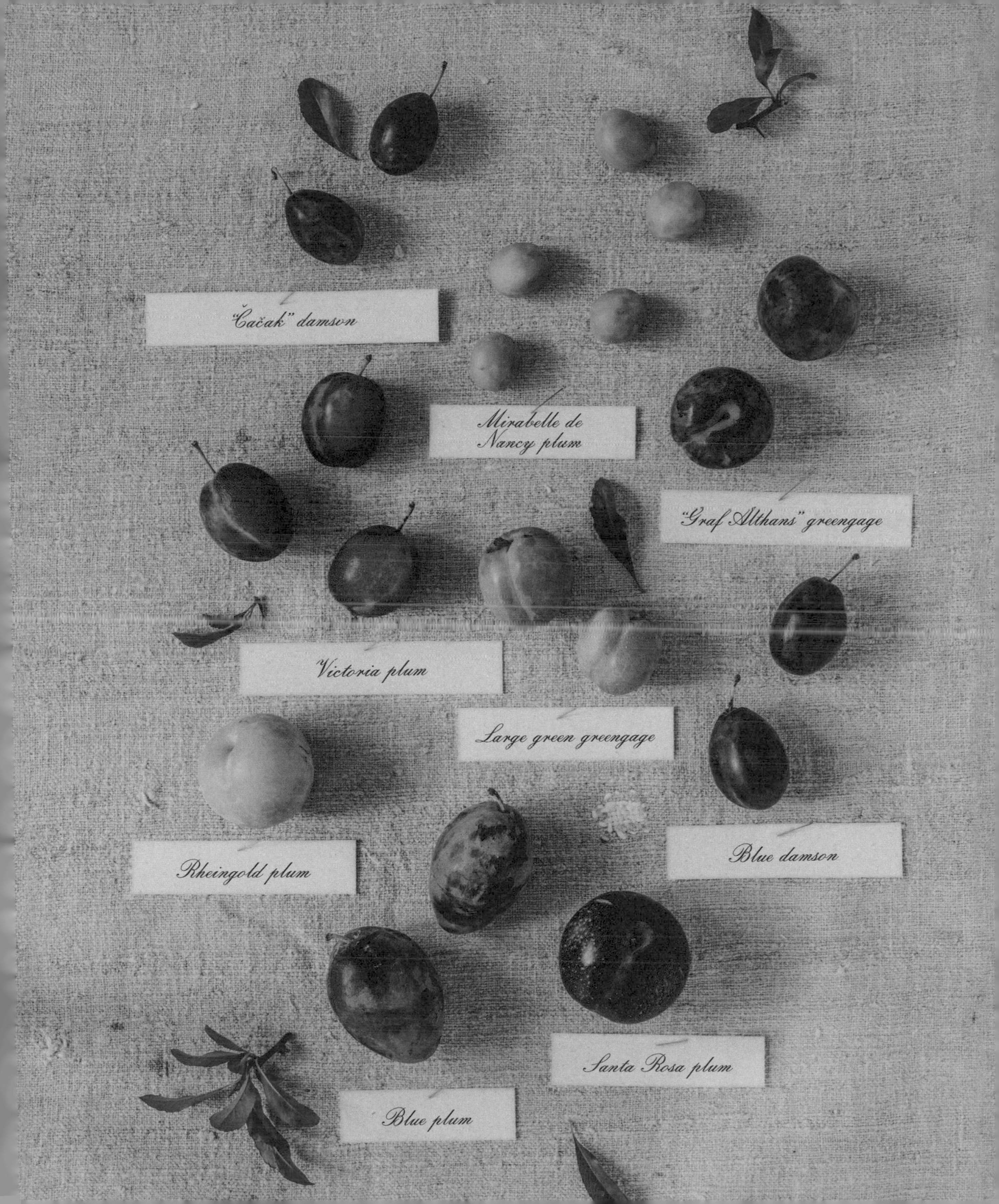

"Čačak" damson

Mirabelle de
Nancy plum

"Graf Althans" greengage

Victoria plum

Large green greengage

Rheingold plum

Blue damson

Santa Rosa plum

Blue plum

BUCKWHEAT MUFFINS

Poppy Seeds & Plums

If you really want to savour the flavours of plum season, these muffins with crunchy oat crumble and poppy seeds are simply perfect. Poppy seeds are highly nutritious and rich in minerals as well as cell-protecting vitamin E. The buckwheat flour adds a nutty element to the muffins.

☞ *MAKES 12 MUFFINS*

CRUMBLE TOPPING

30g (1oz) chilled butter

30g (1oz) jumbo oats
  (gluten-free)

30g (1oz) buckwheat flour

30g (1oz) dark muscovado sugar

½ tsp ground cinnamon

MUFFIN MIX

2 eggs

120g (4¼oz) dark
  muscovado sugar

2–3 drops vanilla extract

100ml (3½fl oz) mild olive oil

175g (6oz) buttermilk

15g (½oz) poppy seeds

150g (5½oz) buckwheat flour

100g (3½oz) cornflour

2 tsp baking powder

pinch of salt

200g (7oz) yellow plums,
  damsons, or Mirabelle plums,
  halved, pitted, and chopped
  into small pieces

Preheat the oven to 180°C (350°F/Gas 4). To make the crumble, work all the ingredients together in a bowl until they resemble crumbs, then set aside.

For the muffin mix, beat the eggs, sugar, and vanilla extract for several minutes in a bowl using an electric whisk until the mixture is pale. Add the oil and buttermilk. In a second bowl, combine the poppy seeds, buckwheat flour, cornflour, baking powder, and salt then add this in batches to the egg and buttermilk mixture.

Carefully fold the fruit into the muffin mixture. Fill the moulds of a muffin tray with 12 paper cases. Divide the mixture evenly between the cases and scatter over the crumble topping. Bake in the centre of the oven for 18–22 minutes, until risen and golden brown. When an inserted wooden skewer comes out clean, they are ready. Leave the muffins to cool on a wire rack.

  15 MINS   *18–22 MINS*

VANILLA TARTLETS

Cherries, Peach, Redcurrants & Pistachio

These exquisite and conveniently sized little tarts are ideal for a summer picnic or as a small snack between meals. The almond-milk custard filling is simple, quick to make, and also vegan. The pistachios add a nutty texture, which goes wonderfully with the summer fruit.

☞ **MAKES 8 TARTLETS (DIAMETER 10CM/8IN)**

SHORTCRUST PASTRY

200g (7oz) spelt flour, plus extra for dusting

50g (1³/₄oz) cornflour

20g (³/₄oz) dark muscovado sugar

½ tsp baking powder

pinch of salt

60ml (2fl oz) mild vegetable oil, plus extra for greasing

baking beans, for blind baking

FILLING

30g (1oz) cornflour

400ml (14fl oz) almond milk

30g (1oz) dark muscovado sugar

1 vanilla pod, halved and seeds removed

TOPPING

2 flat peaches, quartered and cut into very thin slices

24 sweet cherries

8 redcurrant stems

2 tbsp pistachios, chopped

Combine the flour, cornflour, sugar, baking powder, and salt in a bowl. Add the oil and 60ml (2fl oz) cold water, then bring together quickly using your fingers. Avoid overhandling the dough; it should remain fairly rough. Shape it into a ball, wrap in cling film, and rest for 20 minutes in the fridge.

Preheat the oven to 185°C (365°F/Gas 4½). Grease the tartlet tins and dust with flour. Divide the pastry into 8 equal portions and roll each one out into a circle on a floured work surface. Line the tartlet tins with the pastry, press the edges slightly, and trim off any overhanging pastry. Prick the pastry bases several times with a fork and chill for 15 minutes. Cover the pastry with pieces of baking parchment cut to size, weigh each piece down with baking beans, and bake blind for 17–20 minutes in the centre of the oven. Take the tins out of the oven and remove the baking beans and baking parchment. Release the tartlets from their tins and leave to cool completely on a wire rack.

To make the filling, stir the cornflour into 75ml (2½fl oz) of the almond milk until smooth. Put the remaining almond milk, sugar, and the vanilla pod and seeds into a pan and bring to the boil. Add the cornflour paste to the pan, stirring constantly, bring to the boil again, and allow to simmer briefly until the custard thickens. Remove the vanilla pod, pour the custard into the tartlet cases, and leave to cool for 30 minutes.

Arrange the peach slices, 3 cherries, and 1 strand of redcurrants on each tartlet. Scatter with the pistachios and chill for 10 minutes before serving.

  | *20 MINS* *17–20 MINS* ❄ *45 MINS* *30 MINS*

STONE FRUIT CRUMBLE

With Oat & Marzipan Topping

We love summer stoned fruit! It doesn't matter if it's sour cherries, plums, or peaches. In high season, this sensational crumble is a fantastic opportunity to combine these vitamin rich fruits. Energy-packed oat flakes mingle with marzipan and crunchy hazelnuts in the crumble layer.

☞ *MAKES 6–8 PORTIONS*

FRUIT FILLING

1kg (2¼lb) mixed stone fruit (such as sour cherries, peaches, damsons, apricots, or plums), halved

1 apple, coarsely grated

2–3 drops vanilla extract

100ml (3½fl oz) naturally cloudy apple juice

CRUMBLE

50g (1¾oz) hazelnuts, chopped

100g (3½oz) jumbo oats (gluten-free)

150g (5½oz) wholemeal spelt flour

pinch of salt

150g (5½oz) vegan organic marzipan, cut into small cubes

75g (2½oz) mild coconut oil

yogurt, to serve

Preheat the oven to 180°C (350°F/Gas 4). Transfer the stoned fruit to a large casserole dish. Add the grated apple, vanilla extract, and apple juice and bake for 15 minutes. Stir everything once halfway through the cooking time.

Combine the hazelnuts, oats, flour, and salt in a bowl. Add the marzipan along with the coconut oil. Use your fingers to work everything into a crumble. Remove the casserole dish from the oven and scatter the crumble evenly over the fruit. Continue baking in the centre of the oven for 20–25 minutes, until the crumble is golden brown. This dish is best served while still slightly warm. Serve with the yogurt of your choice.

   20 MINS *35–40 MINS*

CRUMBLE FLATBREADS

Gooseberries, Plums & Greengages

At first glance, these crumble flatbreads can appear unremarkable, but eaten warm with an enticing combination of gooseberries, plums, and greengages they are quite simply divine. Spelt crumble and vanilla add the finishing touches to this clever recipe, which is a firm favourite of ours.

☞ *MAKES 6–8 FLATBREADS*

YEAST DOUGH

160ml (5½fl oz) milk of choice – we use almond milk

10g (¼oz) dark muscovado sugar

½ tsp dried yeast

pinch of salt

300g (10oz) spelt flour, plus extra for dusting

FRUIT TOPPING

500g (1lb 2oz) gooseberries, greengages, and plums, mixed

2 tbsp dark muscovado sugar

CRUMBLE

60g (2oz) spelt flour

20g (¾oz) dark muscovado sugar

1–2 drops vanilla extract

30g (1oz) butter

To make the yeast dough, heat the milk until lukewarm. Add the sugar, yeast, and salt and stir well until the yeast has completely dissolved. Use the dough hook on an electric mixer to work the flour into the yeast mixture in a bowl for 2 minutes, until you have a glossy, supple dough. Cover with a tea towel and leave to prove in a warm place for about 1 hour, until doubled in volume.

Meanwhile, line a tray with baking parchment. For the crumble, rub all the ingredients together in a bowl until they form rough crumbs and leave to chill in the fridge.

Knead the yeast dough once again on a floured work surface. Divide the dough into 6–8 portions and roll each one out to create a flatbread (roughly 14 × 8cm/5½ x 3¼in), then place these on the baking tray. Top the dough with a thick layer of fruit (cut surface upwards), then sprinkle with the sugar and crumble. Cover the flatbreads and leave to prove for a further 30 minutes.

Preheat the oven to 200°C (400°F/Gas 6). Bake the flatbreads in the centre of the oven for 12–14 minutes. Serve warm.

 Tip   *For a vegan version, use the same quantity of mild coconut oil instead of the butter.*

① ☕ | 🍶 *20 MINS*   🍞 *12–14 MINS*   💤 *90 MINS*

APRICOT TART

Honey, Lavender & Pine Nuts

This tart tastes like a summer greeting from Provence. Fresh apricots, honey, lavender, and pine nuts conjure up an enticing aroma, which brings back memories of summer holidays in France.

☞ **MAKES 1 TART (DIAMETER 30CM/12IN)**

SHORTCRUST PASTRY

200g (7oz) wholemeal spelt flour (or wholemeal emmer flour), plus extra for dusting

25g (scant 1oz) dark muscovado sugar

pinch of salt

85ml (2¾fl oz) olive oil, plus extra for greasing

1 egg yolk

1 tbsp yogurt of your choice

baking beans, for blind baking

FRUIT FILLING

6–8 sprigs of lavender

2 tbsp pine nuts

1 tbsp mild olive oil

2 tbsp honey

800g (1¾lb) apricots, halved and pitted

1 egg

100g (3½oz) sour cream

ALSO

1 tbsp honey, for drizzling

Combine the flour, sugar, and salt in a bowl. Add the oil, egg yolk, and yogurt and bring together swiftly to make the pastry dough. Avoid overhandling the dough; it should remain fairly rough. Shape it into a ball and roll out between two sheets of cling film into a circle (diameter 36–38cm/14½–15in). Remove the cling film. Grease a tart tin, dust with flour, then line with the pastry. Press the edge down slightly and trim off any overhanging pastry. Prick the pastry base several times with a fork and transfer to the freezer for 30 minutes.

For the filling, shake the sprigs of lavender and strip off the flowers. Heat a large pan. Toast the pine nuts in the dry pan, remove, and set aside. Add the oil, honey, apricots, and lavender flowers, mix carefully, and cook over a low heat for 3 minutes. Leave to cool.

Preheat the oven to 185°C (365°F/Gas 4½). Line the tart case with baking parchment, fill with baking beans, and blind bake for 10 minutes. Take the pastry case out of the oven and remove the baking beans and parchment.

Whisk the egg and sour cream. Spread the egg mixture evenly over the base and top with the apricot mix. Bake the tart for 20–25 minutes in the centre of the oven then remove and leave to cool. Scatter with pine nuts and drizzle honey over the tart to serve.

Tip *Of course, you can also bake this tart using peaches, figs, or grapes.*

  20 MINS *30–35 MINS* 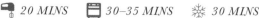 *30 MINS*

BUILDING BLOCKS: BUNDT CAKES

☞ MAKES 1 BUNDT CAKE (DIAMETER 14–16CM/5½–6¼IN, OR 1 ROUND CAKE (DIAMETER 20CM/8IN)

① THE BASIC INGREDIENTS	② TO SWEETEN	③ FAT	④ FLOUR
3 eggs	90g (3¼oz) dark muscovado sugar	85g (3oz) butter	200g (7oz) spelt flour
	or	*or*	*or*
	90g (3¼oz) honey	85g (3oz) mild coconut oil, warmed	100g (3½oz) teff flour + 100g (3½oz) cornflour
	or	*or*	*or*
	90ml (3fl oz) maple syrup	85ml (2¾fl oz) mild vegetable oil	200g (7oz) einkorn flour
			or
			200g (7oz) emmer flour
Preheat the oven to 180°C (350°F/Gas 4). Grease a baking tin (bundt tin diameter 14–16cm/5½–6¼in or springform tin diameter 20cm/8in) and dust with flour. Whisk the eggs in a bowl.	Add the sweetener and whisk well.	Gradually add the fat.	Combine the flour with 2 tsp baking powder and a pinch of salt and add in batches to the cake mix with 100ml (3½fl oz) of your chosen milk.

⑤ SOME FRUIT

150g (5½oz) frozen
cherries, defrosted, or
fresh cherries, stone
removed
or
150g (5½oz) berries
or
150g (5½oz) chopped
apple (about 2 apples)

Fold the fruit into the
cake mixture.

⑥ ADDED FLAVOUR

1 tsp ground cinnamon
or
1–2 drops vanilla
extract
or
pinch of ground black
cardamom seeds

Add the spice and mix
together well.

⑦ A BIT OF CRUNCH

2 tbsp almonds,
chopped
or
2 tbsp hazelnuts,
chopped
or
2 tbsp walnuts, chopped
or
1 tbsp dark chocolate,
chopped

Fold the nuts or
chocolate into the
cake mix and transfer
the mixture to your
tin. Bake the bundt
cake for 50–55 minutes;
or a round cake for
30–35 minutes. Insert a
skewer to test if done.

🖐 | 🥄 *20 MINS*   🍞 *30–35 OR 50–55 MINS*

CHERRY TART

Crunchy Almond Crumble & Vanilla Custard

☞ *MAKES 1 TART*
(DIAMETER
30CM/12IN)

SHORTCRUST PASTRY

150g (5¹/₂oz) teff flour, plus extra
for dusting

75g (2¹/₂oz) cornflour

30g (1oz) dark muscovado sugar

pinch of salt

130g (4³/₄oz) butter, plus extra
for greasing

1 egg

baking beans, for blind baking

FRUIT FILLING

85g (3oz) dried dates, finely
chopped

60g (2oz) custard powder

grated zest and juice of
¹/₂ organic orange

900g (2lb) frozen sour
cherries, thawed

1 vanilla pod, halved lengthways
and seeds removed

CRUMBLE

30g (1oz) gluten-free jumbo oats

15g (¹/₂oz) teff flour

¹/₂ tsp ground cinnamon

25g (scant 1oz) dark
muscovado sugar

30g (1oz) mild coconut oil

30g (1oz) flaked almonds

For the pastry, combine the flour, cornflour, sugar, and salt in a bowl. Add the butter and rub together with your fingers to form fine crumbs. Add the egg and 2 tablespoons of water and work swiftly to create the pastry dough. Avoid overhandling the dough; it should remain fairly rough. Wrap in cling film and chill in the fridge for 30 minutes.

To make the filling, put the dates in a pan with 100ml (3¹/₂fl oz) water, bring to the boil, then simmer gently until soft. Purée and leave to cool. Stir the custard powder into the orange juice until smoothly combined. Bring the puréed dates back to the boil, adding the orange zest, cherries, vanilla pod, and seeds, and simmer gently for 5 minutes. Stir the custard mixture into the hot cherries, bring briefly to the boil, and cook for 1 minute. Remove the vanilla pod and leave the cherry mixture to cool.

To make the crumble, combine the oats, flour, cinnamon, and sugar. Work in the coconut oil, rubbing everything together with your fingers until it forms a crumbly consistency. Fold in the almonds then chill the crumble.

Preheat the oven to 180°C (350°F/Gas 4). Grease the tart tin and dust with flour. Roll out the dough on a floured work surface into a large circle (diameter 36–38cm/14¹/₂–15in). Transfer into the tart tin, press the edge down slightly, and trim off any overhanging pastry. Prick the pastry base several times with a fork and chill for 15 minutes, then line with baking parchment, fill with baking beans, and blind bake in the centre of the oven for 20 minutes. Take the pastry case out of the oven and remove the baking beans and parchment.

Spread the cherry mixture evenly over the pastry and top with the crumble. Bake the tart for 25 minutes, then increase the oven temperature to 200°C (400°F/Gas 6) and bake for a further 5 minutes, until golden brown. Leave to cool on a wire rack then remove from the tin.

  | *35 MINS*  *50 MINS* ❄ *45 MINS*

RASPBERRY AND BLACKBERRY COBBLER

With an Oat and Corn Crust

If you like pies, you will love this cobbler. The term cobbler is indeed linked to the job description "cobbler" and comes from the phrase "to cobble something together". Here, baked sweet fruit is topped with a crisp, golden cornmeal crust, which gives it a distinctive "crunch".

 MAKES 4–6 PORTIONS

FRUIT FILLING

1 apple, roughly grated

300g (10oz) raspberries (fresh or frozen)

300g (10oz) blackberries (fresh or frozen)

1 tsp cornflour

2 tsp lemon juice

1 tsp ground cinnamon

THE COBBLER MIX

60g (2oz) gluten-free jumbo oats

60g (2oz) cornflour

40g (1¼oz) polenta

50g (1¾oz) dark muscovado sugar

1 tsp baking powder

pinch of salt

75g (2½oz) chilled butter

75ml (2½fl oz) almond milk

yogurt, to serve

Preheat the oven to 180°C (350°F/Gas 4). Put the grated apple, raspberries, blackberries, cornflour, lemon juice, and cinnamon in a pan and bring to the boil. Lower the heat and allow the fruit to simmer very briefly. Transfer the fruit to a casserole dish (about 18 × 26cm/7 x 10½in).

Grind the oats in a food processor to make a flour. Combine the ground oats, cornflour, polenta, sugar, baking powder, and salt in a bowl. Add the butter in little blobs and rub everything together with your fingers to create a crumble. Add the almond milk and work this briefly into the mixture until combined. Divide the cobbler mix into 8 equal-sized balls, press each one slightly flat, and arrange them on top of the stewed fruit. Bake the cobbler in the centre of the oven for 35–40 minutes, until golden brown. This dish tastes best slightly warm and served with yogurt of your choice.

Tip *For a vegan version, use the same quantity of mild coconut oil instead of the butter. This recipe also tastes fabulous with other fruits, such as fresh currants, strawberries, or stoned fruits.*

   |  *20 MINS* *35–40 MINS*

OAT WAFFLES

Yogurt & Honey

Oats are rich in vitamins B1 and B6. You can make your own oat flour in no time using a food processor, which can be used to bake fantastic, moist waffles. These waffles are delicious for breakfast, afternoon snacks, or at any time to be honest.

☞ *MAKES ABOUT*
4 WAFFLES (8.5 ×
14CM / 3½ X 5½IN)

BATTER

2 eggs

4 tbsp honey (or maple syrup)

150ml (5fl oz) milk of choice
  – we use almond milk

100g (3½oz) yogurt or
  coconut yogurt

200g (7oz) jumbo oats
  (gluten-free)

1 tsp ground cinnamon

2 tsp baking powder

pinch of salt

oil for the waffle iron

fresh fruit, yogurt, or other
  toppings (see p.60), to serve

Beat the eggs, honey, milk, and yogurt in a bowl using an electric whisk. Grind the oats in a food processor to make a flour. In a second bowl, combine the ground oats, cinnamon, baking powder, and salt. Add this to the milk mixture and mix everything gently.

Oil and preheat the waffle iron. For each waffle, put 2 tablespoons of batter onto the iron and cook until golden. Continue in this way until all the batter has been used. Serve with fresh fruit, yogurt, or the topping of your choice (see Tip p.60).

 10 MINS   *12 MINS*

BLUEBERRY PANCAKES

Light Batter & Buttermilk

These American-style pancakes are very light and fluffy thanks to the buttermilk and whisked egg whites, while the blueberries add a sweet, fruity element. This recipe is bound to become one of your all-time classic favourites for Sunday breakfasts.

 MAKES 8–10 PANCAKES

BATTER

3 eggs

125g (4½oz) buttermilk

110g (3¾oz) spelt, emmer, or einkorn flour, or 90g (3¼oz) gluten-free flour mix

2 tsp baking powder

pinch of salt

some oil for the pan

200g (7oz) blueberries

DECORATION

blueberries and phlox flowers (optional)

Separate the eggs. Beat the egg yolks with the buttermilk in a bowl using an electric whisk. In a second bowl, combine your chosen flour with the baking powder. Add this to the milk mixture and stir everything gently to form a thick batter. Whisk the egg whites with the salt until stiff and carefully fold this into the batter using a balloon whisk.

Heat some oil in a large pan and add 1–2 tablespoons of batter for each pancake, scatter over a few blueberries, and cook for 2–3 minutes, until golden brown and firm underneath. Flip the pancakes and continue cooking until the other side is also nice and golden. Continue in this way until all the batter has been used, keeping the cooked pancakes warm as you work. Scatter the blueberries over the pancakes and, if using, decorate with the flowers.

Tip *These pancakes taste best drizzled with some maple syrup. Instead of blueberries, the pancakes also taste fabulous with bananas, chopped apple, or other berries.*

Elderberries

Wild
strawberries

Cranberries

Blackcurrants

Red raspberries

White currants

Yellow
raspberries

Blueberries

Blackberries

Redcurrants

Wild blueberries

Gooseberries

Strawberries

Lingonberries

RICOTTA CHEESECAKE

Biscuit Base, Banana & Raspberry Coulis

The world-famous New York cheesecake was invented in 1872 by William Lawrence from Chester, New York. With just a couple of simple tweaks you can bake a slightly lighter, less sweet version. Ripe bananas, ricotta, and sour cream ensure a creamy consistency.

☞ *MAKES 1 CAKE (DIAMETER 20CM/8IN)*

BASE

150g (5¹/₂oz) spelt or wholemeal biscuits

75g (2¹/₂oz) butter, melted

CHEESECAKE FILLING

1 large ripe banana, mashed

500g (1lb 2oz) ricotta

250g (9oz) sour cream

75g (2¹/₂oz) acacia honey

grated zest of ½ organic lemon

1 tbsp cornflour

3 eggs

RASPBERRY COULIS

150g (5¹/₂oz) frozen raspberries, defrosted

1–2 drops vanilla extract

2 tbsp acacia honey

DECORATION

100g (3¹/₂oz) raspberries,

50g (1³/₄oz) redcurrants (optional)

Put the biscuits in a freezer bag and gently bash with a rolling pin to form crumbs. Combine the biscuit crumbs and butter in a bowl. Line a springform tin (diameter 20cm/8in) with baking parchment, tip the crumbs into the tin, carefully press them flat to make the base, and chill briefly in the fridge.

Preheat the oven to 150°C (300°F/Gas 2). Beat together the mashed banana, ricotta, sour cream, honey, lemon zest, and cornflour in a bowl, then stir in the eggs, one at a time. Fill a heatproof dish with water and place this on the bottom of the oven. Transfer the cheesecake mixture into the tin and bake in the centre of the oven for 55–60 minutes, until the filling has set. When you shake the tin gently you should still see a bit of a "jelly wobble". Leave the cheesecake to cool completely.

Remove the cheesecake from the tin. To make the coulis, purée the frozen raspberries, vanilla, and honey and drizzle over the cheesecake. Decorate the cheesecake with the raspberries and, if using, the redcurrants.

🖟 *20 MINS*   🍞 *55–60 MINS*

BLACKBERRY BUNDT CAKE

Cardamom & Blueberry Icing

In summer we love collecting wild blackberries while out cycling, then once back at home we use the fruit to try out new recipes. One of these is this bundt cake made using chickpea flour. The flour is very rich in protein and its excellent baking properties help to make the cake wonderfully moist.

 MAKES 1 BUNDT CAKE (DIAMETER 14–16CM/5½–6¼IN)

CAKE MIX

3 eggs

120ml (4fl oz) maple syrup

125ml (4¼fl oz) mild vegetable oil

1–2 drops vanilla extract

½ tsp black cardamom seeds

120g (4¼oz) chickpea flour

130g (4¾oz) teff flour

3 tsp baking powder

pinch of salt

150ml (5fl oz) almond milk

100g (3½oz) blackberries (fresh or frozen)

coconut oil and polenta for greasing and dusting

ICING

1 quantity cashew icing (see page 193)

2 tsp blueberry fruit powder

DECORATION

75g (2½oz) blackberries

Preheat the oven to 180°C (350°F/Gas 4). Beat the eggs and maple syrup in a bowl for several minutes with an electric whisk, gradually adding the oil and vanilla extract. Finely grind the cardamom using a pestle and mortar. In a second bowl, combine both types of flour, the cardamom, baking powder, and salt. Add this to the egg mixture, alternating with the almond milk until everything is well mixed. Carefully fold the blackberries into the cake mixture.

Grease a bundt tin with coconut oil and dust with polenta. Transfer the cake mixture to your tin and bake in the centre of the oven for 1 hour, until risen and golden brown. When an inserted wooden skewer comes out clean, the bundt cake is ready. Leave to cool in the tin for about 10 minutes, then turn out onto a wire rack and leave to cool completely.

Colour the cashew icing with the blueberry fruit powder and ice the bundt cake. Wash and dab dry the blackberries and decorate the cake.

Tip   *Instead of blackberries, you could also try making this bundt cake using the same quantity of blueberries. To make sure the decorative blackberries stay in place, you can secure them using toothpicks that have been cut in half.*

20 MINS | *1 HR*

BLACKCURRANT SPIRALS

Wholegrain Emmer, Vanilla & Honey

Of all the berries, we think blackcurrants are the unsung stars – their exceptional flavour is absolutely unique. They also provide plenty of vitamin C and have anti-inflammatory properties. Here the blackcurrants are given centre stage in these crisp, yet soft, spirals.

☞ *MAKES 12 SPIRALS*

YEAST DOUGH

300ml (10fl oz) milk of choice
– we use almond milk

50g (1³/₄oz) dark
muscovado sugar

2–3 drops vanilla extract

8g dried yeast

pinch of salt

500g (1lb 2oz) wholemeal
emmer flour, plus extra
for dusting

80g (2³/₄oz) softened butter, plus
extra for greasing

FILLING

300g (10oz) blackcurrants,
stalks removed
(or redcurrants)

60g (2oz) acacia honey

To make the yeast dough, heat the milk in a pan until lukewarm. Add the sugar, vanilla, yeast, and salt and stir well until the yeast has completely dissolved. Use the dough hook attachment on an electric mixer to combine the flour with the milk mixture and the butter in a bowl for a couple of minutes, until you have a glossy and supple dough. Cover with a tea towel and leave to prove in a warm place for 1 hour, until doubled in volume.

Grease the moulds of a muffin tray and dust with flour. Knead the dough thoroughly on a floured work surface and roll it out into a rectangle (about 28 x 38cm/11 x 15in). Scatter the dough with blackcurrants and drizzle over the honey. Roll up the rectangle from the long side and slice the roll into 12 sections. Place each piece into a muffin tray mould. Cover with a tea towel and leave to prove in a warm place for a further 30 minutes.

Preheat the oven to 220°C (425°F/Gas 7). Bake the spirals in the centre of the oven for 8–10 minutes then remove and leave to cool on a wire rack.

 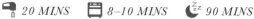 *20 MINS* *8–10 MINS* *90 MINS*

LATE SUMMER BERRY GATEAU

Light Sponge, Citrus Notes & a Medley of Berries

At the height of summer, the different berry bushes in the garden virtually explode with fruit. The perfect dish for this time is our berry gateau with its light sponge, low-fat curd cheese, and colourful berries If you like berries, you're going to be thrilled with this recipe.

☞ **MAKES 1 CAKE (DIAMETER 20CM/8IN)**

SPONGE

5 eggs

80g (2³/₄oz) dark muscovado sugar

grated zest of ½ organic orange

pinch of salt

75g (2½oz) ground almonds

75g (2½oz) cornflour

2 tsp baking powder

butter and cornflour for greasing and dusting

FILLING

320g (11oz) low-fat quark

175g (6oz) full-fat cream cheese

1 tsp cornflour

1 tsp icing sugar

3 tbsp maple syrup

2–3 drops vanilla extract

grated zest of ½ organic lemon

250g (9oz) mixed berries

DECORATION

150g (5½oz) mixed berries and blackberry flowers (optional)

Preheat the oven to 190°C (375°F/Gas 5). Separate the eggs. In a bowl, beat the egg yolks and 60g (2oz) of the sugar with 10 tablespoons of water and the orange zest using an electric whisk until thick and foamy. Whisk the egg whites with the salt until stiff, trickling in the remaining sugar as you go. Gently fold the whisked egg whites into the yolk and sugar mixture. In another bowl, combine the almonds, cornflour, and baking powder and sift this over the egg mixture. Fold in briefly using a balloon whisk.

Grease just the bases of two springform tins (diameter 20cm/8in) with butter and dust with cornflour. Divide the cake mix equally between the tins, smooth the surface, and bake in the centre of the oven for 18–22 minutes, until the cakes have risen and are golden brown in colour. When an inserted wooden skewer comes out clean, they are ready. Release the cakes from the tins and leave to cool completely on a wire rack.

To make the filling, stir together all the ingredients except the berries. Place one of the cakes on a cake platter. Spread two-thirds of the cream over this base. Cover with berries, then put the second cake on top and spread over the remaining cream. Decorate the cake, as desired, with berries and blackberry flowers. Chill in the fridge for 30–60 minutes before serving.

 ⊟ 25 MINS   ⊟ 18–22 MINS   ❄ 30–60 MINS

SPELT WAFFLES

Belgium-style

These wholesome waffles with fresh berries are perfect for breakfast or for a weekend afternoon tea. Our version of these Belgium-style yeasted waffles uses nutritious spelt flour and substitutes dark muscovado sugar for the traditional pearl sugar.

☞ **MAKES ABOUT 8 WAFFLES (8.5 × 14CM / 3½ X 5½IN)**

BATTER

125g (4½oz) butter, plus extra for greasing

250ml (4fl oz) milk of choice – we use almond milk

4g dried yeast

60g (2oz) dark muscovado sugar

2 eggs

200g (7oz) wholemeal spelt flour

200g (7oz) spelt flour

2–3 drops vanilla extract

1 tsp ground cinnamon

1 tsp baking powder

pinch of salt

selection of fresh fruit, to serve

DECORATION

blackberry flowers (optional)

Melt the butter in a pan over a moderate heat. Add the milk and 200ml (7fl oz) water, heat until lukewarm, and remove from the hob. Dissolve the yeast and sugar in the lukewarm liquid.

Separate the eggs. In a bowl, combine both types of flour, the cinnamon, and baking powder. Add the milk mixture, egg yolks, and vanilla extract, and use an electric whisk to create a smooth batter. In a separate bowl, whisk the egg whites with the salt until stiff and carefully fold into the waffle mixture using a balloon whisk. Cover with a tea towel and leave to stand in a warm place for 20 minutes.

Grease and preheat the waffle iron. For each waffle, put 2 tablespoons of the batter onto the iron and cook until golden. Continue in this way until all the batter has been used. Fresh fruit is the perfect accompaniment with these waffles. If you wish, decorate with blackberry flowers.

 Tip   *These waffles can also be cooked ahead of time and frozen. Heat them up individually in the toaster – they will taste as good as when freshly cooked.*

🖳 *10 MINS*   ▦ *24 MINS*   💤 *20 MINS*

BLUEBERRY GALETTE

Delicate Yogurt Shortcrust & Hints of Citrus

In August, we love to pick homegrown blueberries from pick-your-own farms that grow this superfood. Once you are back home, making this warm tart can be your reward. These super berries are also rich in vitamins, minerals, and other important micronutrients.

☞ *MAKES 1 GALETTE*

SHORTCRUST BASE

225g (8oz) wholemeal einkorn flour, plus extra for dusting

70g (2¼oz) polenta

30g (1oz) dark muscovado sugar

pinch of salt

90g (3¼oz) chilled butter

50g (1¾oz) yogurt of choice

FRUIT TOPPING

450g (1lb) blueberries

2 tsp cornflour

25g (scant 1oz) dark muscovado sugar

2–3 drops vanilla extract

grated zest and 1 tbsp juice of ½ organic lemon

ALSO

2 tbsp milk of choice

1 tsp dark muscovado sugar

yogurt or vanilla ice cream, to serve

Preheat the oven to 200°C (400°F/Gas 6). Combine the flour and polenta with the sugar and salt in a bowl. Add the butter in little blobs and rub the ingredients with your fingers until combined. Avoid overhandling the dough; the texture should remain fairly rough. Stir the yogurt into 70ml (2½fl oz) water, add to the bowl, and work quickly into the other ingredients. Wrap in cling film and chill in the fridge for 20 minutes.

Meanwhile, mix the blueberries with the remaining topping ingredients.

Dust a piece of baking parchment with the flour and roll out the shortcrust into a large disc (diameter about 28cm/11in). Use the baking parchment to transfer the pastry onto a baking tray. Spread the filling out in the centre, leaving a 3cm (1½in) border around the edge. Fold up the edges of the pastry over the filling and press gently into place. Brush the edge with milk and sprinkle with the sugar. Bake the galette in the centre of the oven for 25–30 minutes, until golden brown. The galette tastes best served warm with yogurt or a scoop of vanilla ice cream.

 Tip   *Of course, this recipe also works with frozen blueberries, too. Just defrost the berries beforehand and let them drain.*

   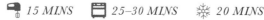 *15 MINS*   *25–30 MINS*   ❄ *20 MINS*

BLACKBERRY SWISS ROLL

Almond Sponge & Vanilla-Quark Cream

Swiss roll is an absolute classic and hugely popular with us. We use almond flour here because it retains plenty of moisture, which gives the sponge an excellent texture. A light quark cream together with jam, fresh berries, and flowers add the finishing touches to this violet summer dream.

☞ **MAKES 1 SWISS ROLL (8–10 PIECES)**

SPONGE

5 eggs

80g (2³/₄oz) dark muscovado sugar, plus extra for coating

2–3 drops vanilla extract

pinch of salt

80g (2³/₄oz) almond flour

50g (1³/₄oz) cornflour

FILLING

2–3 drops vanilla extract

2 tbsp maple syrup

400g (14oz) low-fat quark

50g (1³/₄oz) whipping cream

1 tsp cornflour

1 tsp icing sugar

250g (9oz) blackberries

75g (2¹/₂oz) blackberry jam, 70 per cent fruit content

DECORATION

75g (2¹/₂oz) blackberries and blueberries, mixed

purple basil leaves and sweet William flowers (optional)

Preheat the oven to 190°C (375°F/Gas 5). Separate the eggs. In a bowl, beat the egg yolks and 60g (2oz) of the sugar with 10 tablespoons of water and the vanilla extract using an electric whisk, until thick and foamy. Whisk the egg whites with the salt until stiff, trickling in the remaining sugar as you go. Combine the almond flour and cornflour in another bowl. Carefully fold the whisked egg whites into the egg-yolk mixture with a balloon whisk. Sift over the flour mixture and quickly fold this in, too. Line a baking tray with baking parchment. Spread the sponge mixture over the tray to make a roughly 34 × 34cm (13 x 13in) square. Bake in the centre of the oven for 9–11 minutes, until the sponge has risen and is golden yellow.

Place a clean tea towel that is larger than your sponge on the work surface and sprinkle evenly with sugar. Turn the cooked sponge out onto a board and carefully peel off the baking parchment, then tip the sponge onto the prepared tea towel so that the smooth sponge base is in contact with the towel. Trim the sponge all around to straighten the edges. Swiftly roll up the sponge with the tea towel while the sponge is still warm and leave to cool like this.

Stir the vanilla extract and maple syrup into the quark until smooth. Beat the cream with the cornflour and icing sugar until it holds its shape, and fold this into the quark. Gently unroll the sponge and spread with a layer of jam followed by the cream, leaving a 1cm (¹/₂in) border free at the edges. Scatter over the blackberries. Roll up the sponge once again, using the tea towel to help you, and slide the cake onto a plate with the seam facing down.

Decorate the Swiss roll with berries and, if you wish, scatter with basil leaves and flowers. Chill for 30 minutes before serving.

  25 MINS    9–11 MINS   ❊ 30 MINS

BLACKBERRY CHEESECAKES

Wholemeal Biscuit Base & Blackberry Coconut Cream

Ripe blackberries are super juicy and full of vitamins, not to mention low in calories, and they have a sweet and sour flavour. We've captured their enticing forest flavour in this light, airy cheesecake. The fruity quark and coconut cream sits on a crunchy wholemeal biscuit base, which doesn't require any baking.

☞ *MAKES 4 CHEESECAKES (DIAMETER 8CM/3¼IN)*

BASES

80g (2¾oz) wholemeal biscuits

40g (1¼oz) butter, melted

CREAMY TOPPING

400g (14oz) low-fat quark

80g (2¾oz) frozen blackberries, defrosted, or fresh blackberries

60g (2oz) acacia honey

2–3 drops vanilla extract

grated zest and 2 tbsp juice from 1 organic lime

100ml (3½fl oz) coconut milk

1 tsp cornflour

1 tsp icing sugar

DECORATION

75g (2½oz) blackberries,

blackberry flowers (optional)

Put the wholemeal biscuits into a freezer bag and bash gently with a rolling pin to form crumbs. Combine the biscuit crumbs and butter in a bowl. Place four food presentation rings (diameter 8cm/3¼in) on a flat dish lined with baking parchment. Put a quarter of the biscuit crumb mix into each ring, carefully pressing each base flat, then transfer to the fridge.

For the creamy topping, use a hand-held blender to purée the quark, blackberries, honey, vanilla extract, and lime zest and juice in a high-sided container. Gently heat the coconut milk in a pan, add the corn flour and icing sugar, and stir. Add spoonfuls of the blackberry mixture to the coconut milk mixture until the temperatures are roughly equal. Then stir both mixtures together. Transfer the cream into the pre-prepared moulds and chill in the fridge for 2 hours, until the topping has set.

To serve, release the cheesecakes from the ring moulds, arrange on a plate, and, if you wish, decorate with blackberries and blackberry flowers.

Tip *You could also prepare these cheesecakes in glasses or small bowls.*

🔨 *20 MINS* ❄ *2 HRS*

BLUEBERRY NAKED CAKE

Hazelnut Sponge, Coconut Cream & Blueberry Jam

☞ *MAKES 1 CAKE (DIAMETER 20CM/8IN)*

JAM

150g (5½oz) frozen or fresh
    blueberries

25g (scant 1oz) dark
    muscovado sugar

CAKE MIX

100g (3½oz) hazelnuts

4 eggs

70g (2¼oz) dark
    muscovado sugar

100ml (3½fl oz) mild vegetable
    oil, plus extra for greasing

100g (3½oz) apple purée
    (see page 192)

2–3 drops vanilla extract

160g (5¾oz) wholemeal emmer
    flour or wholemeal spelt,
    plus extra for dusting

3 tsp baking powder

pinch of salt

100ml (3½fl oz) almond milk

FILLING

double quantity of coconut
    cream recipe (see page 193)

200g (7oz) blueberries

DECORATION

edible flowers: horned violets,
    borage, purple basil (optional)

Bring the blueberries and sugar to the boil in a pan. Lower the heat and simmer the berries for a couple of minutes, until the liquid has reduced and the consistency resembles thick jam. Stir occasionally during cooking, then leave the jam to cool.

Toast the hazelnuts in a dry pan until pale brown. Leave to cool completely before grinding finely in a food processor.

Preheat the oven to 185°C (365°F/Gas 4½). Beat the eggs and sugar in a bowl for several minutes with an electric whisk, until the mixture is a pale cream colour. Add the oil, apple purée, and vanilla extract and stir. In a second bowl, combine the hazelnuts, flour, baking powder, and salt and add this in batches to the egg mixture, alternating with the milk. Take care not to stir too much once combined.

Grease two springform tins (diameter 20cm/8in) with oil and dust with the flour. Divide the cake mixture equally between the tins, smooth the surface, and bake in the centre of the oven for 20–25 minutes, until risen and golden. When an inserted wooden skewer comes out clean, the cakes are ready. Remove the cakes from the tins and leave to cool completely on a wire rack.

Briefly chill the coconut cream for the filling. Place one of the cakes on a cake platter. Roughly fold the jam into the coconut cream using a spatula and spread half the mixture over the cake. Spread half the blueberries over the cream, place the second cake on top, and cover with the remaining blueberry and coconut cream. Scatter over the remaining blueberries and decorate the cake as desired with edible flowers. Chill in the fridge for 30–60 minutes before serving.

🕸 | 🖛 *25 MINS*　📟 *20–25 MINS*　❄ *30–60 MINS*

BERRY PIZZA

Ricotta, Acacia Honey & Pine Nuts

This fantastic sweet pizza made using a crunchy spelt dough is not only utterly delicious, the baking process is really fun, too! Spread with a bit of ricotta then feel free to finish it off as you please with a selection of healthy berries. A bit of honey adds a subtle sweetness and mint gives it a fresh zing.

☞ *MAKES 1 PIZZA (DIAMETER 28CM/11IN)*

YEAST DOUGH

100ml (3¹/₂fl oz) milk of choice – we use almond milk

15g (¹/₂oz) dark muscovado sugar

5g dried yeast

pinch of salt

190g (6¹/₂oz) spelt flour, plus extra for dusting

1¹/₂ tbsp mild olive oil

FRUIT TOPPING

300g (10oz) mixed berries (blueberries, raspberries, blackcurrants, redcurrants, white currants)

85g (3oz) ricotta

2–3 tbsp acacia honey

2 tbsp pine nuts

a few mint leaves

To make the yeast dough, heat the milk in a pan until lukewarm. Add the sugar, yeast, and salt and stir everything well. Put the flour and oil into a bowl. Add the milk mixture and use the dough hook attachment on an electric mixer to process everything for a few minutes, until you have a glossy, supple dough. Cover with a tea towel and leave to prove in a warm place for 1 hour, until doubled in volume.

Meanwhile, set aside a few of the berries for decorating. Line a tray with baking parchment and preheat the oven to 200°C (400°F/Gas 6).

Knead the yeast dough once again on a floured work surface and roll it out to create a circle (diameter 28cm/11in), shaping the edges to come up slightly higher. Lay the dough on a baking tray, spread ricotta evenly over the surface, and top with a densely packed layer of berries. Drizzle with honey and scatter over the pine nuts. Bake the pizza in the centre of the oven for 20–23 minutes. Remove from the oven and scatter over the mint leaves and reserved berries.

  20 MINS   20–23 MINS   1 HR

ELDERBERRY GATEAU

Dark Chocolate, Cardamom & Coconut Cream

☞ *MAKES 1 CAKE (DIAMETER 20CM/8IN)*

COMPOTE

1 tsp cornflour

¼ tsp black cardamom seeds

150g (5½oz) elderberries, stalks removed

50g (1¾oz) acacia honey

CAKE MIX

100g (3½oz) dark chocolate, 70 per cent cocoa content

4 eggs

150g (5½oz) acacia honey

100g (3½oz) mild coconut oil, plus extra for greasing

2–3 drops vanilla extract

160g (5¾oz) wholemeal einkorn flour, plus extra for dusting

70g (2¼oz) ground almonds

3 tsp baking powder

pinch of salt

100ml (3½fl oz) milk of choice – we use almond milk

FILLING

1 quantity coconut cream recipe (see page 193)

DECORATION

75g (2½oz) blackberries, edible flowers, purple basil leaves (optional)

To make the compote, stir the cornflour into 3½ tablespoons of water. Finely grind the cardamom seeds using a pestle and mortar. Bring the elderberries, cardamom, and honey to the boil in a pan and simmer briskly for 1–2 minutes. Add the cornflour mixture, stirring constantly, and bring to the boil briefly until the compote has thickened slightly. Set aside and leave to cool.

Preheat the oven to 180°C (350°F/Gas 4). Roughly chop the chocolate and melt over a bain-marie. Beat the eggs and honey for several minutes in a bowl with an electric whisk until the mixture is a pale cream colour. Gradually add the coconut oil and vanilla extract. In a second bowl, combine the flour, almonds, baking powder, and salt and add this in batches to the egg mixture, alternating with the milk. Take care not to stir too much once combined. Stir in the melted chocolate.

Grease two springform tins (diameter 20cm/8in) with coconut oil and dust with flour. Divide the cake mixture equally between the tins, smooth the surface, and bake in the centre of the oven for 20–25 minutes, until risen and golden brown. When an inserted wooden skewer comes out clean, the cakes are ready. Leave to cool on a wire rack. Briefly chill the coconut cream.

Once the cakes are cool, place one of them on a cake platter and spread with half the coconut cream. Cover this with about two-thirds of the compote and place the second cake on top. Finally add the remaining coconut cream followed by the remaining compote. Decorate the gateau as desired with blackberries, edible flowers, and basil. Chill for 30–60 minutes before serving.

Tip   *If you can't get hold of elderberries, you can make the gateau with frozen sour cherries or cranberries.*

 🍶 *25 MINS*   🍴 *20–25 MINS*   ❄ *30–60 MINS*

A RICH HARVEST

As the dahlias come into bloom, we head slowly into autumn. The last of the blackberries gladden our hearts, while plump, rosy-cheeked apples, colourful pears, golden quinces, and sweet late-season plums are just waiting to be harvested and complemented with wonderful flavours.

"SAVE A BANANA" PANCAKES

Wholemeal Spelt Flour & Walnuts

Of all fruit, overripe bananas are the most likely to end up in the bin. This pancake recipe is great for exploiting the sweetness of fully ripe bananas and avoiding waste. You can also use overripe bananas in our moist banana bread (see page 166).

 MAKES 8 PANCAKES

BATTER

1 large ripe banana, mashed

1 egg

200ml (7fl oz) milk of choice – we use almond milk

25g (scant 1oz) mild coconut oil, warmed, plus extra for cooking

1–2 drops vanilla extract

125g (4½oz) wholemeal spelt flour

½ tsp ground cinnamon

½ tsp baking powder

50g (1¾oz) walnuts, roughly chopped

Combine the mashed banana with the egg, milk, coconut oil, and vanilla extract using an electric whisk. In a second bowl, combine the flour, cinnamon, and baking powder. Add this to the banana mixture and stir gently to create a thick, smooth batter. Fold the walnuts into the batter.

Heat some coconut oil in a pan and add 1½–2 tablespoons of batter for each pancake. Cook for 2–3 minutes, until the underside is golden and firm, then flip the pancakes and continue cooking until the other side is also nice and golden. Continue in this way until all the batter has been used. Keep the cooked pancakes warm as you work.

Tip   *The pancakes taste best warm, drizzled with some maple syrup. Fresh fruit such as figs or berries also go beautifully.*

HAZELNUT BUNDT CAKE
Maple Syrup & Beetroot Icing

Marbled bundt cakes are a regular feature at our house. This version uses hazelnuts that have been roasted and ground, giving the cake a very intense nutty flavour. With its colourful beetroot icing and berry topping, this classic recipe has become a favourite cake for birthdays!

☞ **MAKES 1 BUNDT CAKE (DIAMETER 22CM/8½IN)**

CAKE MIX

200g (7oz) hazelnuts

250g (9oz) softened butter, plus extra for greasing

150ml (5fl oz) maple syrup

5 eggs

2–3 drops vanilla extract

250g (9oz) spelt flour, plus extra for dusting

5 tsp baking powder

pinch of salt

150ml (5fl oz) milk of choice – we use almond milk

1 tbsp rum

ICING

1 quantity cashew icing (see page 193)

2 tsp beetroot powder

DECORATION

50g (1¾oz) blackberries

30g (1oz) blueberries

Toast the hazelnuts in a dry pan until pale brown then leave to cool completely. Finely grind 150g (5½oz) of the hazelnuts in a food processor, chop the remaining hazelnuts, and set both aside.

Preheat the oven to 180°C (350°F/Gas 4). Cream the butter in a bowl with an electric whisk for several minutes until pale. Stir in the maple syrup, the eggs, one at a time, and the vanilla extract. In a second bowl, combine the flour, ground and chopped hazelnuts, baking powder, and salt. Add this in batches to the egg mixture, alternating with the milk and rum and mixing gently.

Grease a bundt tin (diameter 22cm/8½in) with butter and dust with the flour. Transfer the cake mixture to the tin and bake in the centre of the oven for 50 minutes to 1 hour, until risen and golden brown. When an inserted wooden skewer comes out clean, the bundt cake is ready. Leave the bundt cake to cool in the tin for about 10 minutes, then turn it out onto a wire rack and leave to cool completely.

Colour the cashew icing with the beetroot powder and use to ice the bundt cake. Decorate the cake with the berries.

 Tip *To make sure the blackberries stay in place, you can secure them using toothpicks that have been cut in half.*

🔌 *20 MINS*   🍞 *50–60 MINS*

PLUM CAKE

Cinnamon & Vanilla Crumble

This tray bake brings back unforgettable childhood memories of the plum harvest in our grandmother's garden. Baking this classic together was an annual ritual. Our updated version is crammed with plums and is less sweet, while the cinnamons gives it a sophisticated twist.

 MAKES 1 TRAY BAKE

YEAST DOUGH

200ml (7fl oz) milk of choice – we use almond milk

25g (scant 1oz) dark muscovado sugar

10g (¼oz) dried yeast

pinch of salt

375g (13oz) spelt flour, plus extra for dusting

50g (1¾oz) softened butter

FRUIT TOPPING

1.5kg (3lb 3oz) plums

1 tbsp dark muscovado sugar

2 tsp ground cinnamon

CRUMBLE

100g (3½oz) spelt flour

30g (1oz) dark muscovado sugar

2–3 drops vanilla extract

60g (2oz) chilled butter

DECORATION

phlox flowers (optional)

To make the yeast dough, heat the milk in a pan until lukewarm. Add the sugar, yeast, and salt and stir well. Use the dough hook on an electric mixer to combine the flour, yeast mixture, and butter in a bowl for a couple of minutes, until you have a glossy, supple dough. Cover with a tea towel and leave the dough to prove in a warm place for 1 hour, until doubled in volume.

Meanwhile, for the crumble, rub all the ingredients together in a bowl until you have rough crumbs and leave to chill in the fridge.

Knead the yeast dough once again on a floured work surface and roll it out to the size of your tray. Transfer onto a tray lined with baking parchment. Cover the dough with a closely packed layer of plums (cut surface facing up) and scatter with the sugar, ground cinnamon, and the crumble. Cover the cake and leave to prove once more for 30 minutes.

Preheat the oven to 180°C (350°F/Gas 4). Bake the plum cake in the centre of the oven for 35–40 minutes then remove and leave to cool. If you wish, decorate with phlox flowers.

Tip　*For a vegan version, you can replace the butter with the same quantity of coconut oil and use a plant-based milk. This cake also tastes great with other varieties of plums or with chopped apple.*

   | *30 MINS* *35–40 MINS* 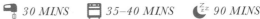 *90 MINS*

BLUEBERRY "FRANZBRÖTCHEN"

Cardamom, Vanilla & Dates

"Franzbrötchen", a traditional speciality in Hamburg, Germany, are made using puff pastry or a yeast-leavened dough and are often served with coffee. Traditionally, the filling is packed with fat and sugar; our version is baked using a juicy blueberry filling and has a hint of cardamom.

☞ *MAKES 12 BUNS*

YEAST DOUGH

300ml (10fl oz) milk of choice
  – we use almond milk

½ tsp black cardamom seeds

50g (1¾oz) dark
  muscovado sugar

1 tsp ground cinnamon

7g dried yeast

pinch of salt

500g (1lb 2oz) spelt flour, plus
  extra for dusting

75g (2½oz) softened butter

FILLING

75g (2½oz) dried dates,
  chopped

250g (9oz) frozen blueberries
  (ideally wild)

1 tsp ground cinnamon

1–2 drops vanilla extract

grated zest of ½ organic lemon

To make the yeast dough, heat the milk in a pan until lukewarm. Grind the cardamom seeds using a pestle and mortar. Add the cardamom, sugar, cinnamon, yeast, and salt to the milk and stir well until the yeast has completely dissolved. Use the dough hook attachment on an electric mixer to combine the flour with the milk mixture and the butter in a bowl for a couple of minutes, until you have a glossy and supple dough. Cover with a tea towel and leave to prove in a warm place for 1 hour, until doubled in volume.

Meanwhile, for the filling, place the dates in a pan with 2 tablespoons of water, bring them to the boil, then simmer until soft. Purée and leave to cool. Bring the blueberries to the boil in another pan and simmer down until the juice has almost completely evaporated. Stir in the date purée, cinnamon, vanilla extract, and lemon zest and leave to cool.

Knead the dough thoroughly on a floured work surface and carefully roll it out into a rectangle (about 30 x 40cm/12 x 15½in). Cover the dough evenly with the filling. Roll up the rectangle from the long side and slice the roll into 12 sections. Place the swirls onto two trays lined with baking parchment, cover with tea towels, and leave to prove in a warm place for a further 30 minutes.

Preheat the oven to 220°C (425°F/Gas 7). Bake each tray of swirls in the centre of the oven for 8–10 minutes.

 Tip   *For a vegan version, you can use the same quantity of mild coconut oil instead of the butter and a plant-based milk instead of cow's milk.*

  15–20 MINS   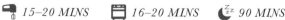 *16–20 MINS*   *90 MINS*

BUCKWHEAT BUNDT CAKE

Cranberries & Dark Chocolate

In the Celle region in Lower Saxony, Germany, buckwheat cake with lingonberries is a real classic, but cranberries are a good substitute. Here we have reinterpreted the traditional recipe in bundt cake form. The cranberries keep the buckwheat sponge moist, a chocolate glaze adds the finishing touch, and the whole cake is crowned with fresh figs.

☞ *MAKES 1 BUNDT CAKE (DIAMETER 22CM/8½IN)*

CAKE MIX

5 eggs

150g (5½oz) dark muscovado sugar

250ml (9fl oz) mild vegetable oil, plus extra for greasing

2–3 drops vanilla extract

175g (6oz) buckwheat flour, plus extra for dusting

75g (6oz) cornflour

150g (5½oz) ground hazelnuts

5 tsp baking powder

pinch of salt

175ml (6fl oz) almond milk

200g (7oz) frozen cranberries, thawed

50g (1¾oz) dark chocolate, 70 per cent cocoa content, roughly chopped

ALSO

30g (1oz) dark chocolate, 70 per cent cocoa content, roughly chopped

3 fresh figs, quartered

Preheat the oven to 180°C (350°F/Gas 4). Beat the eggs and sugar in a bowl for several minutes with an electric whisk, gradually adding the oil and vanilla extract as you go. In a second bowl, combine the flour, cornflour, hazelnuts, baking powder, and salt. Add this in batches to the egg mixture, alternating with the milk and mixing everything gently. Add the chocolate to the mixture, carefully folding it in along with the cranberries.

Grease a bundt tin (diameter 22cm/8½in) with oil and dust with the flour. Transfer the cake mix into the tin and bake in the centre of the oven for 50–55 minutes, until risen and golden brown. When an inserted wooden skewer comes out clean, the bundt cake is ready. Leave to cool in the tin for about 10 minutes, then turn out onto a wire rack and leave to cool completely.

To make the icing, melt the chocolate over a bain-marie. Decorate the bundt cake with the chocolate glaze and arrange the figs on top.

 Tip

To make a lactose-free version, you can use vegan dark chocolate. Instead of cranberries, you could also use sour cherries. To make sure the decorative figs stay in place, you can secure them using toothpicks that have been cut in half.

  |  *20 MINS* 🗔 *50–55 MINS*

"Celler Dickstiel"

Red-fleshed

Red Boskoop

Idared

"Wellant"

"Delbarestivale"

Ananas Reinette

Elstar

Glockenapfel

"Roter Imperiale"

Pinova

APPLE CAKE

Ginger, Cloves & Cinnamon

Apple cake is one of our absolute favourites. It brings back reassuring childhood memories of Sunday afternoon tea with granny in the autumn, making the most of the apple harvest from the garden. Our version is made with einkorn flour, maple syrup, warming spices, and lots of apple.

☞ *MAKES 1 CAKE (DIAMETER 26CM/10½IN)*

CAKE MIX

3 eggs

pinch of salt

120g (4½oz) softened butter, plus extra for greasing

150ml (5fl oz) maple syrup, or 150g (5½oz) dark muscovado sugar

seeds from 1 vanilla pod

300g (10oz) einkorn flour, plus extra for dusting

pinch of ground ginger

pinch of ground cloves

1 tsp ground cinnamon, plus extra for sprinkling

2 tsp baking powder

150ml (5fl oz) almond milk

1 tbsp rum

ALSO

750g (1lb 10oz) apples (about 4 apples), peeled, quartered, and cored

2 tbsp apricot jam, 70 per cent fruit content

Preheat the oven to 185°C (365°F/Gas 4½). Separate the eggs. Beat the egg whites and salt in a bowl with an electric whisk until stiff. In another bowl, cream the butter for several minutes until pale, then add the maple syrup and egg yolks, stir everything together, then add the vanilla seeds. Combine the flour, spices, and baking powder and gradually add to the mix, alternating with the almond milk and rum and mixing everything gently. Finally, gently fold in the egg whites with a balloon whisk. Make parallel incisions in each apple quarter.

Grease a springform tin (diameter 26cm/10½in) and dust with some of the flour. Transfer the mixture into the tin, smooth the surface, and arrange the apple quarters on top. Bake the cake in the centre of the oven for 40–45 minutes, until risen and golden brown. When an inserted wooden skewer comes out clean, the cake is ready. Leave the cake to cool in the tin for about 10 minutes, then turn out onto a wire rack and leave to cool completely.

Heat the apricot jam in a pan over a low heat and use this to brush the cake while it is still warm. Finally, sprinkle with a little cinnamon and leave to cool on a wire rack.

🔨 *20 MINS*   🍳 *40–45 MINS*

APPLE CRUMBLE MUFFINS

Cinnamon, Ginger & Marzipan Crumble

In this recipe we combine two popular classics – apple crumble and American muffins – with nutritious spelt flour and marzipan crumble. A hint of ground ginger lends a touch of sophistication. These muffins taste absolutely fantastic eaten while still slightly warm.

☞ MAKES 12 MUFFINS

CRUMBLE TOPPING

90g (3¼oz) spelt flour

10g dark muscovado sugar

40g (1¼oz) chilled butter

30g (1oz) organic marzipan

MUFFIN MIX

2 eggs

175g (6oz) buttermilk

100ml (3½fl oz) mild vegetable oil

2–3 drops vanilla extract

120g (4¼oz) dark muscovado sugar

225g (8oz) spelt flour

2 tsp baking powder

½ tsp ground cinnamon

pinch of ground ginger

pinch of salt

200g (7oz) apples (about 2 apples), peeled, quartered, cored, and chopped into small pieces

Preheat the oven to 180°C (350°F/Gas 4). To make the crumble, rub all the ingredients together in a bowl to form crumbs, then set aside.

For the muffin mix, whisk the eggs, buttermilk, oil, and vanilla extract in a bowl. In a second bowl, combine the sugar, flour, baking powder, cinnamon, ground ginger, and salt. Add the wet ingredients to the dry and beat briefly using an electric whisk, until the mixture is smooth and silky.

Fill the moulds of a muffin tray with 12 paper cases. Carefully fold the chopped apple into the muffin mix and divide the mixture evenly between the cases. Partially bake the muffins in the centre of the oven for 8 minutes, remove from the oven, and scatter over the crumble topping. Continue cooking the muffins for another 12–14 minutes, until risen and golden brown. When an inserted wooden skewer comes out clean, they are ready. Leave the muffins to cool on a wire rack.

🔨 *25 MINS*   🍳 *20–22 MINS*

BLACKBERRY AND APPLE PIE

Crunchy Spelt Pastry & Cinnamon

Blackberries and apples are like Ginger Rogers and Fred Astaire: they complement each other perfectly and are a guaranteed box-office hit. The apples are slightly more dominant in terms of taste, while the sweet and tangy blackberries add flavour and give the pie filling its deep red colour.

☞ *MAKES 1 PIE (DIAMETER 24CM/9½IN)*

SHORTCRUST PASTRY

350g (12oz) spelt flour, plus extra for dusting

pinch of salt

160g (5¾oz) chilled butter, plus extra for greasing

2 tbsp maple syrup

1 egg

2 tbsp milk of choice – we use almond milk

FILLING

1kg (2¼lb) apples (about 6 apples), peeled

250g (9oz) blackberries

85g (3oz) dark muscovado sugar

1–2 drops vanilla extract

1 tsp ground cinnamon

grated zest and 1 tbsp juice from 1 organic lemon

ALSO

1 egg yolk

1 tbsp milk of choice – we use almond milk

1 tbsp dark muscovado sugar

yogurt, to serve

Combine the flour and salt in a bowl. Add the butter in little blobs and rub everything with your fingers to form fine crumbs. Add the maple syrup, egg, and milk and work in swiftly. Avoid overhandling the pastry; it should remain fairly rough. If it looks too dry, add a bit more milk. Wrap the pastry in cling film and chill in the fridge for 30 minutes.

Roughly grate one apple. Quarter the others, remove the cores, then slice each quarter in half lengthways. Combine the chopped and grated apple with the blackberries, sugar, vanilla extract, cinnamon, and lemon juice and zest.

Preheat the oven to 180°C (350°F/Gas 4). Grease a tart tin (diameter 24cm/9½in) and dust with the flour. Roll out half the pastry on a floured work surface into a circle (diameter 30–34cm/12–13in). Transfer into the tart tin, press the edge down slightly, and trim off any overhanging pastry. Tip the filling into the pastry case and brush the pastry rim with a bit of water. Roll out the remaining pastry, slice into 4–5cm (1¾–2in) wide strips, and place these in a braided pattern on the filling. Trim any overhanging pastry strips, pressing the ends down firmly on the rim of the pie. Use your thumb and index finger to create a wave pattern around the edge of the pastry. Whisk the egg yolk and milk and use this to brush over the pie then sprinkle with the sugar. Bake the pie in the centre of the oven for 40–45 minutes, until golden brown. This tastes best while still warm and served with yogurt.

Tip *Instead of using fresh blackberries, the recipe also works well with fresh raspberries or defrosted and well-drained berries.*

  30 MINS *40–45 MINS*  *30 MINS*

RAISIN BREAD

Moist Spelt Yeast Dough & a Hint of Orange

Raisins contain lots of minerals and B-group vitamins so they are brilliant for combating physical exhaustion and stress. They taste particularly great in this classic north German recipe. In our version we soak the raisins beforehand in orange juice so the bread is extra moist.

☞ *MAKES 1 LOAF*
(25 × 11CM/
10 X 4½IN)

YEAST DOUGH

200g (7oz) raisins

200ml (7fl oz) orange juice

250ml (9fl oz) milk of choice –
   we use almond milk, plus
   extra for brushing

2 tsp acacia honey

20g (¾oz) dried yeast

pinch of salt

300g (10oz) spelt flour, plus
   extra for dusting

200g (7oz) wholemeal
   spelt flour

50g (1¾oz) softened butter, plus
   extra for greasing

1 egg

Soak the raisins in the orange juice for 1 hour. Pour off the juice and leave to drain well.

To make the yeast dough, heat the milk in a pan until lukewarm. Add the honey, yeast, and salt and stir well until the yeast has completely dissolved. Use the dough hook attachment on an electric mixer to combine both types of flour with the yeast mixture, butter, and egg for a couple of minutes, until you have a glossy and supple dough. Work the raisins into the dough. Cover with a tea towel and leave to prove in a warm place for 1 hour, until doubled in volume.

Grease a loaf tin (11 × 25cm/10 x 4½in) with butter and dust with the flour. Knead the yeast dough once again on a floured work surface, shape it into a 25cm (10in) long roll, and transfer to the tin. Cover with a tea towel and leave to prove in a warm place for a further 30 minutes to 1 hour, until it has significantly increased in volume.

Preheat the oven to 180°C (350°F/Gas 4). Brush the raisin bread with milk and make a roughly 1cm (½in) deep incision lengthways along the loaf. Bake in the centre of the oven for about 40 minutes, until risen and golden brown. After baking, let the raisin bread stand in the tin on a wire rack for about 10 minutes, then run a knife round the bread, tip it out of the tin, and leave to cool completely.

Tip *If you don't like raisins, you could replace them with dried cranberries or sour cherries. Currants and sultanas are also great options. Make sure you buy unsulphured dried fruit.*

  20 MINS   40 MINS   ᶻᶻ 2½–3 HRS

MINI CHOCOLATE CAKES

Molten Centre, Dates & Raspberry Coulis

Dark chocolate with a high cocoa content inhibits the release of stress hormones thanks to the flavonoids it contains, which means it has a calming effect. So every now and then we love to treat ourselves to this pure indulgence with its molten centre, sweet dates, and fresh autumn fruits.

 MAKES 6 MINI CAKES

CAKE MIX

100g (3¹/₂oz) dried dates, finely chopped

100g (3¹/₂oz) dark chocolate, 70 per cent cocoa content, roughly chopped

1 tbsp cocoa powder, plus extra for dusting

2–3 drops vanilla extract

60g (2oz) mild coconut oil, plus extra for greasing

2 eggs

30g (1oz) chickpea flour

RASPBERRY COULIS

150g (5¹/₂oz) frozen raspberries, defrosted

¹/₂ tbsp dark muscovado sugar

ALSO

75g (2¹/₂oz) blackberries

40g (1¹/₄oz) blueberries

6 figs, stalks removed

1 tbsp pomegranate seeds

purple basil leaves and flowers (optional)

dark chocolate, 70 per cent cocoa content (optional)

Place the dates in a pan with 75ml (2¹/₂fl oz) water, bring them to the boil, then simmer gently until soft. Purée and leave to cool.

Preheat the oven to 180°C (350°F/gas 4). Melt the chocolate over a bain-marie along with the cocoa powder, vanilla extract, and coconut oil, stirring thoroughly. Leave the mixture to cool slightly.

Beat the eggs in a bowl with an electric whisk for several minutes, then add the date and chocolate mixture and stir. Finally, add the chickpea flour and continue to stir briefly. Grease the moulds of a muffin tray with coconut oil and dust with cocoa powder. Divide the mixture evenly between the moulds and bake in the centre of the oven for 10–12 minutes, until risen.

Meanwhile, for the coulis, purée the raspberries with the sugar and push the mixture through a sieve. Make a cross-shaped incision in each fig and press it open like a crown. Serve the warm mini chocolate cakes immediately with the raspberry coulis, berries, and figs. If you wish, decorate with pomegranate seeds, basil leaves, and flowers, plus some grated chocolate.

Tip   *To make a lactose-free version, you can use vegan dark chocolate.*

   20 MINS   *10–12 MINS*

PLUM AND POPPY SEED TART

Crisp Spelt Shortcrust & Vanilla-Quark Filling

This tart is reminiscent of a favourite dish from our childhood days: quark soufflé with plums. We've packaged up the whole combination with a new twist to include poppy seeds and a vanilla custard – all in a heavenly tart with spelt shortcrust, light, low-fat quark, and a delicate hint of citrus.

☞ *MAKES 1 TART (DIAMETER 30CM/12IN)*

SHORTCRUST PASTRY

200g (7oz) wholemeal spelt flour or wholemeal emmer or einkorn, plus extra for dusting

30g (1oz) dark muscovado sugar

pinch of salt

100g (3½oz) chilled butter, plus extra for greasing

1 egg

baking beans, for blind baking

FILLING

300g (10oz) low-fat quark

100g (3½oz) full-fat cream cheese

3 eggs

grated zest of 1 organic lemon

75g (2½oz) acacia honey

60g (2oz) custard powder

20g (¾oz) poppy seeds

500g (1lb 2oz) plums or damsons, halved and stones removed

Combine the flour, sugar, and salt in a bowl. Add the butter in little blobs and rub everything together with your fingers to form fine crumbs. Add the egg and work in swiftly. Avoid overhandling the pastry; it should remain fairly rough. Wrap in cling film and chill in the fridge for 30 minutes.

To make the filling, mix all the ingredients (except the plums) until the consistency is smooth and creamy.

Preheat the oven to 180°C (350°F/Gas 4). Grease a tart tin (diameter 30cm/12in) and dust with the flour. Roll out the pastry on a floured work surface into a large circle (diameter 36–38cm/14–15in). Transfer into the tart tin, press the edge down slightly, and trim off any overhanging pastry. Prick the pastry base several times with a fork and chill for 15 minutes. Line the pastry with baking parchment, fill with baking beans, and bake blind in the centre of the oven for 20 minutes. Take the pastry case out of the oven and remove the baking beans and baking parchment.

Spread the quark mixture evenly over the base and top with the plums, packed in close together (cut surface facing up). Cook the tart for 30–35 minutes, until done. Leave to cool before serving.

Tip   *Instead of standard plums, you can also use other varieties of plum such as greengages or Mirabelle plums.*

🍽 | 🎛 *30 MINS*   🍳 *50–55 MINS*   ❄ *45 MINS*

CHICKPEA PANCAKES

Bay Leaf-Infused Pears & Almonds

If you enjoy pancakes for Sunday breakfast during the autumn months, you will absolutely love this version with bay leaf-infused stewed pears and almonds. The chickpea flour makes the pancakes crisp on the outside and soft on the inside – and they are really filling.

☞ *MAKES 16–18 PANCAKES*

BATTER

85g (3oz) jumbo oats (gluten-free)

2 eggs

1 tbsp dark muscovado sugar

250ml (9fl oz) almond milk

2 tbsp mild coconut oil, warmed, plus extra for cooking

2–3 drops vanilla extract

90g (3¼oz) chickpea flour

1 tsp ground cinnamon

1 tsp baking powder

pinch of salt

ALSO

30g (1oz) almonds

2 tbsp mild coconut oil

2 ripe, but still firm, pears (such as Williams), quartered and cored

2 fresh bay leaves

200g (7oz) blackberries

maple syrup (optional)

Grind the oats in a food processor to form a flour. Whisk together the eggs, sugar, milk, oil, and vanilla extract in a bowl. In another bowl, combine the ground oats, chickpea flour, cinnamon, baking powder, and salt. Add this to the egg mixture and beat everything using an electric whisk until you have a thick, smooth batter.

Toast the almonds in a dry pan over a moderate heat until pale brown. Remove from the pan and set aside. Heat the oil in the pan and add the quartered pears and bay leaves. Cook over a moderate heat for 4–5 minutes, turning the pears occasionally. Remove from the pan and set aside, remembering to remove the bay leaves before eating.

Heat some more oil in the pan and add 2 tablespoons of the batter for each pancake. Cook for 2–3 minutes, until the underside looks golden brown and firm, then flip the pancakes and continue cooking until the other side is also golden. Continue in this way until all the batter has been used, keeping the cooked pancakes warm as you work.

Serve the pancakes with the bay-leaf infused pears and blackberries. Roughly chop the toasted almonds and scatter over and, if you wish, drizzle the pancakes with maple syrup.

 20 MINS   🍳 *25 MINS*

GRAPE CALZONE

Honey, Olive Oil & Rosemary

A trip to Tuscany inspired us to create this recipe. The combination of sweet Chianti grapes with rosemary and olive oil is really popular there. In this rustic calzone made using spelt flour, the earthy flavour of rosemary blends perfectly with the sweetness of the grapes and honey.

MAKES 6 CALZONE

YEAST DOUGH

150ml (5fl oz) milk of choice
 – we use almond milk

25g (scant 1oz) dark
 muscovado sugar

4g dried yeast

pinch of salt

250g (9oz) spelt flour, plus
 extra for dusting

2 tbsp mild olive oil, plus extra
 for brushing

FILLING

360g (12½oz) black grapes,
 halved lengthways and
 deseeded

2 sprigs of rosemary

1 tbsp mild olive oil

1 tbsp white wine

1 tbsp acacia honey

grated zest of 1 organic lemon

DECORATION

sprig of rosemary, stems
 removed, needles finely
 chopped

To make the yeast dough, heat the milk in a pan until lukewarm. Add the sugar, yeast, and salt and stir well until the yeast has completely dissolved. Use the dough hook on an electric mixer to combine the flour, yeast mixture, and oil in a bowl for a couple of minutes, until you have a glossy, supple dough. Cover with a tea towel and leave to prove in a warm place for 1 hour, until doubled in volume.

Meanwhile, mix the grapes with the remaining filling ingredients.

Knead the dough again on a floured work surface and divide into 6 equal-sized portions. Shape these into balls and roll them out into circles (diameter about 15cm/6in). Spread some of the filling over half of each circle, leaving at least 1cm (½in) free at the edge. Fold the pastry over the filling to create a semicircle shape. Press the air out from the centre towards the edge, press down firmly all the way round, and crimp the edges to ensure the dough parcels are well-sealed. Transfer onto a tray lined with baking parchment, cover with a tea towel, and leave to prove in a warm place for a further 30 minutes. Decorate some of the calzone parcels with rosemary needles.

Preheat the oven to 200°C (400°F/Gas 6). Brush the calzone with a bit of oil and bake in the centre of the oven for 10–12 minutes.

Tip   *To make a vegan version, the acacia honey can be replaced by the same quantity of maple syrup and the cow's milk with a plant-based milk.*

   20 MINS   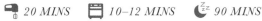 *10–12 MINS*   *90 MINS*

UPSIDE-DOWN CAKE
Figs & Hazelnuts

Figs might seem a little exotic but new varieties are becoming available that can temporarily withstand temperatures of minus 20 degrees, which means they can be cultivated in colder climes. We love this low-calorie fruit, which delivers dietary fibre along with vitamins and minerals.

 MAKES 1 CAKE (DIAMETER 26CM/10½IN)

CAKE MIXTURE

120g (4½oz) dark muscovado sugar

160g (5¾oz) apple purée (see page 192)

160ml (5½fl oz) almond milk

1 tbsp cider or red wine vinegar

1 tsp ground cinnamon

300g (10oz) spelt flour, plus extra for dusting

100g (3½oz) ground hazelnuts or almonds

5 tsp baking powder

pinch of salt

7 figs (about 400–450g/ 14oz–1lb), stalks removed, cut into 7mm (⅓in) thick slices

vegetable oil, for the tin

coconut yogurt, to serve

Preheat the oven to 180°C (350°F/Gas 4). In a bowl, briefly whisk the sugar, apple purée, almond milk, vinegar, and cinnamon using an electric whisk. In a second bowl, combine the flour, hazelnuts, baking powder, and salt, taking care to mix thoroughly. Add the liquid ingredients to this bowl and mix everything swiftly until you have a smooth consistency.

Grease a springform tin (diameter 26cm/10½in) with oil and dust with the flour. Arrange the sliced figs on the base of the springform tin. Spread the cake mix over the top and bake in the centre of the oven for 30–35 minutes, until risen and golden brown. When an inserted wooden skewer comes out clean, the cake is ready. Remove the fig cake from the oven, leave to cool slightly, then release from the tin and leave to cool upside down on a wire rack. This goes beautifully with coconut yogurt.

Tip *You can also make this upside-down cake outside of fig season using halved apricots, plums, or slices of pear.*

  15 MINS  *30–35 MINS*

Williams

Comice

Santa Maria

Alexander Lucas

Gute Luise

Conference

Beurre Hardy

Abate Fetel

Apple quince

Pear quince

QUINCE RYE CAKE

Blackberries & Walnuts

Thankfully the once overlooked quince is now being rediscovered. It is low in calories, rich in vitamin C, and was held in high regard by our grandmothers, who would have used it to make quince cheese and quince cake. Here we combine it with blackberries and walnuts to make a really special tray bake.

☞ *MAKES 1 TRAY BAKE*

YEAST DOUGH

200ml (7fl oz) milk of choice
— we use almond milk

25g (scant 1oz) dark
moscovado sugar

10g (¼oz) dried yeast

pinch of salt

200g (7oz) spelt flour, plus extra
for dusting

175g (6oz) rye flour

50g (1¾oz) softened butter

FRUIT TOPPING

½ vanilla pod, sliced lengthways
and seeds removed

250ml (9fl oz) naturally cloudy
apple juice

3 tbsp maple syrup (or honey)

1 cinnamon stick

4 cloves

¼ tsp black cardamom seeds

grated zest and 3 tbsp juice from
1 organic lemon

1kg (2¼lb) quinces, peeled,
quartered, and sliced into
segments

250g (9oz) blackberries (fresh or
frozen and thawed)

30g (1oz) walnuts

To make the yeast dough, heat the milk in a pan until lukewarm. Add the sugar, yeast, and salt and stir well until the yeast has completely dissolved. Use the dough hook attachment on an electric mixer to combine both types of flour with the yeast mixture and the butter in a bowl for a couple of minutes, until you have a glossy and supple dough. Cover with a tea towel and leave to prove in a warm place for 1 hour, until doubled in volume.

Meanwhile, add the vanilla pod and seeds to a pan with the apple juice, 250ml (9fl oz) water, maple syrup, spices, and lemon zest and juice and bring to the boil. Add the quinces and simmer for 10 minutes, until soft, then leave to drain. Retain the cooking liquid and simmer down until you have about 125ml (4¼fl oz).

Preheat the oven to 185°C (365°F/Gas 4½). Knead the yeast dough once more on a floured work surface and roll it out to the size of your tray. Transfer it onto the tray, lined with baking parchment, and top with a closely packed layer of quince slices. Drizzle with half the cooking liquid. Part-bake in the centre of the oven for 15 minutes. Remove the cake from the oven and scatter over the walnuts and blackberries, then continue baking for another 20 minutes. Remove from the oven, drizzle over the remaining cooking liquid, and leave to cool.

Tip *For a vegan version, use the same quantity of mild coconut oil instead of the butter.*

  35 MINS   35 MINS   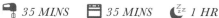 1 HR

PEAR AND WALNUT BUNDT CAKE

Einkorn, Cardamom & Cinnamon

Walnuts are packed with potassium and zinc and their slightly bitter flavour goes beautifully with the vitamin-rich, sweet pears. When these two are combined with einkorn flour, the result is a moist cake, which will no doubt become a firm favourite. A nice hot cup of tea provides the perfect accompaniment.

☞ *MAKES 1 BUNDT CAKE (DIAMETER 22CM/8½IN)*

CAKE MIXTURE

5 eggs

150g (5½oz) dark muscovado sugar

250ml (9fl oz) mild vegetable oil, plus extra for greasing

½ tsp black cardamom seeds

400g (14oz) einkorn flour, plus extra for dusting

1 tsp ground cinnamon

5 tsp baking powder

pinch of salt

150ml (5fl oz) milk of choice – we use almond milk

1 tbsp rum

2 pears, about 200g (7oz), peeled, cored, and chopped into small pieces

50g (1¾oz) walnuts, chopped

ICING

1 quantity cashew icing (see page 193)

DECORATION

walnuts, horned violets, purple basil leaves (optional)

Preheat the oven to 180°C (350°F/Gas 4). Beat the eggs and sugar in a bowl for several minutes with an electric whisk, gradually adding the oil as you go. Finely grind the cardamom using a pestle and mortar. In a second bowl, combine the cardamom, flour, cinnamon, baking powder, and salt, then add this in batches to the egg mixture, alternating with the milk and rum. Mix everything gently. Fold the chopped pear and nuts gently into the cake mixture.

Grease a bundt tin (diameter 22cm/8½in) with oil and dust with the flour. Transfer the mixture to your tin and bake in the centre of the oven for 50 minutes to 1 hour, until risen and golden brown When an inserted wooden skewer comes out clean, the bundt cake is ready.

Leave to cool in the tin for about 10 minutes, then turn out onto a wire rack and leave to cool completely. Cover with the cashew icing and, if you wish, decorate with walnut kernels, horned violets, and basil leaves.

Tip *You can also make a version of this bundt cake using chopped quince. Other nuts such as hazelnuts or almonds work well, too.*

Ⓣ | 🔨 *15 MINS*   🔲 *50–60 MINS*

QUINCE GALETTES

Crunchy Hazelnut Shortcrust & Apple Purée

Not only do quinces have a unique flavour, they also have an unrivalled, aromatic scent with hints of citrus, pear, and apple. This low-calorie fruit will strengthen your immune system thanks to the valuable nutrients it contains. These French-style galettes are made using teff flour and hazelnuts and are simple yet simultaneously sophisticated.

☞ *MAKES 8 GALETTES*

SHORTCRUST PASTRY

150g (5^1/$_2$oz) teff flour, plus extra
    for dusting

100g (3^1/$_2$oz) cornflour

50g (1^3/$_4$oz) ground hazelnuts

25g (scant 1oz) dark
    muscovado sugar

pinch of salt

90g (3^1/$_4$oz) chilled butter

70g (2^1/$_4$oz) buttermilk

1 egg

FRUIT TOPPING

300g (10oz) quinces, peeled,
    quartered, and cored

300g (10oz) apple purée
    (see page 192)

GLAZE

1 tsp cornflour

60ml (2fl oz) naturally cloudy
    apple juice

pinch of ground cinnamon

1–2 drops vanilla extract

Combine the teff flour, cornflour, hazelnuts, sugar, and salt in a bowl. Add the butter in little blobs and rub everything together with your fingers to form fine crumbs. Add the buttermilk and egg and work in swiftly. Avoid overhandling the pastry; it should remain fairly rough. Wrap in cling film and chill in the fridge for 20 minutes.

Meanwhile, for the topping, slice the quince very thinly using a potato peeler.

Preheat the oven to 185°C (365°F/Gas 4^1/$_2$). On a floured work surface divide the pastry into 8 equal-sized portions and shape each into a ball. Roll out the balls to make circles (diameter 14cm/5^1/$_2$in) and place them on two baking trays lined with baking parchment. Put a portion of apple purée on each galette, leaving a 1cm (^{1}/$_2$in) border free around the edge. Top with the sliced quince, overlapping the pieces in the shape of a rosette. Fold the edges of the pastry over the filling and press gently into place. Bake each tray of galettes in the centre of the oven for 25–30 minutes, until golden brown, then remove from the oven.

For the glaze, mix the cornflour with 1 tablespoon of the apple juice. Bring the remaining apple juice, cinnamon, and vanilla extract to the boil in a pan. Add the cornflour paste while stirring constantly and continue to simmer briefly until the glaze has thickened. Brush the glaze over the galettes while they are still warm and serve.

Tip *Of course, this recipe also tastes great with apple or pear slices.*

25 MINS   *50–60 MINS*   *20 MINS*

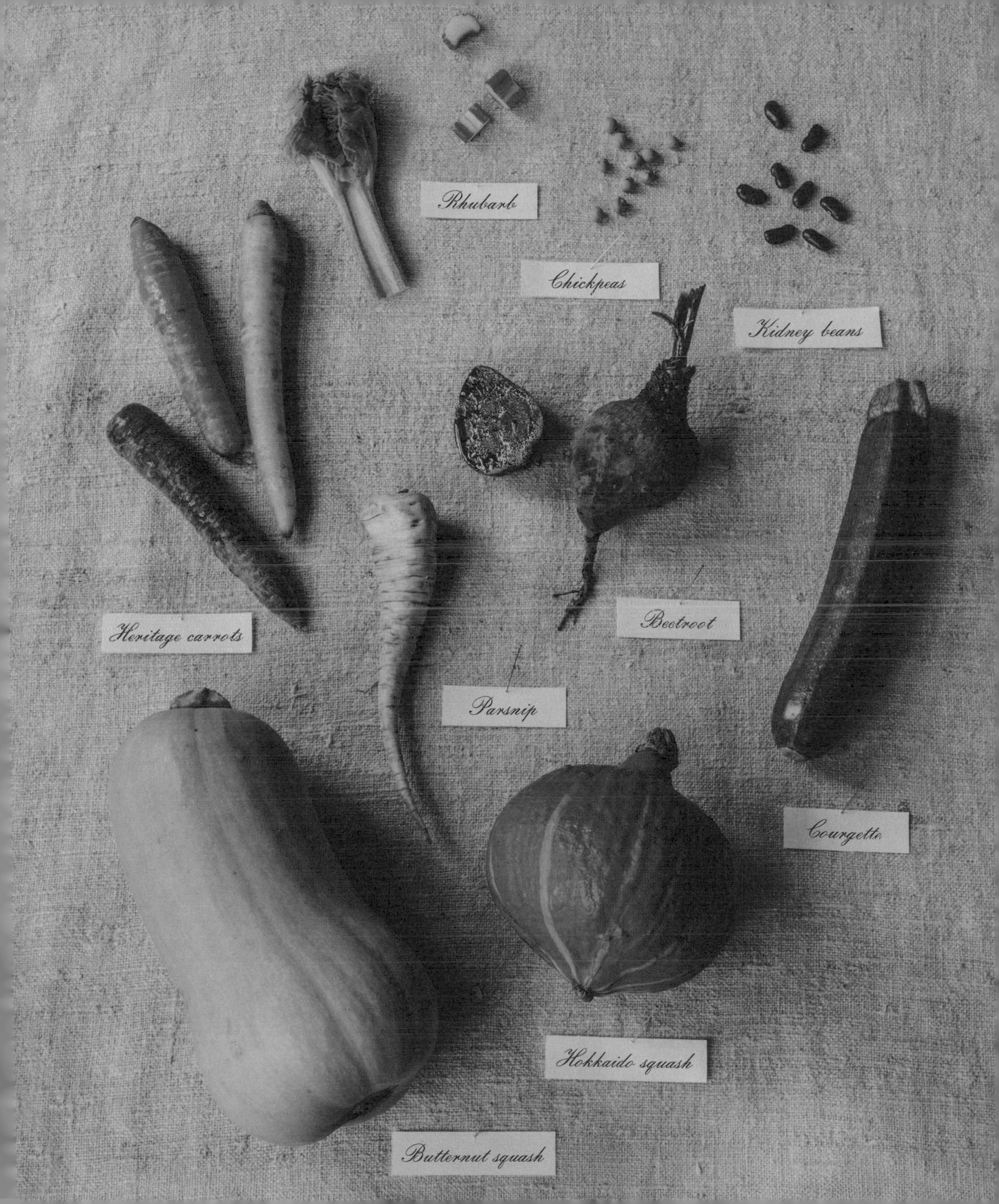

Rhubarb

Chickpeas

Kidney beans

Heritage carrots

Beetroot

Courgette

Parsnip

Hokkaido squash

Butternut squash

PARSNIP CAKE

Coconut, Raisins & Cream Cheese Topping

Parsnips are usually cooked in savoury dishes and are not often used as an ingredient in baking. Nevertheless, this vegetable, which is rich in the micronutrients niacin and potassium, has a perfect flavour for sweet cakes.

☞ *MAKES 1 CAKE (DIAMETER 20CM/8IN)*

CAKE MIXTURE

125g (4¹/₂oz) mild coconut oil, plus extra for greasing

2 eggs

150g (5¹/₂oz) dark muscovado sugar

2–3 drops vanilla extract

175g (6oz) wholemeal einkorn flour, plus extra for dusting

50g (1³/₄oz) desiccated coconut

1 tsp ground cinnamon

1 tsp mixed spice

2 tsp baking powder

pinch of salt

175ml (6fl oz) milk of choice – we use almond milk

1 tbsp rum

175g (6oz) parsnips, peeled and finely grated

70g (2¹/₄oz) raisins

TOPPING

200g (7oz) full-fat cream cheese

3 tbsp runny honey

30g (1oz) mild coconut oil

grated zest of 1 organic lemon

2 tbsp toasted coconut flakes

Preheat the oven to 185°C (365°F/Gas 4¹/₂). Gently melt the coconut oil in a pan over a low heat. Beat the eggs and sugar in a bowl for several minutes with an electric whisk, gradually adding the coconut oil and vanilla extract as you go. In another bowl, combine the flour, desiccated coconut, spices, baking powder, and salt. Add this in batches to the egg and oil mixture, alternating with the milk and rum and stirring everything gently. Fold the grated parsnip and raisins into the cake mix.

Grease a springform tin (diameter 20cm/8in) with coconut oil and dust with the flour. Transfer the cake mix into the tin, smooth the surface, and bake in the centre of the oven for 35–40 minutes, until risen and golden brown. When an inserted wooden skewer comes out clean, the cake is ready. Leave the cake to cool in the tin for about 10 minutes, then turn out onto a wire rack and leave to cool completely.

To make the topping, briefly beat the cream cheese, honey, coconut oil, and lemon zest with an electric whisk until creamy. Spread the cream evenly over the cake and sprinkle with coconut flakes.

🍶 | 🔌 *25 MINS* 🍱 *35–40 MINS*

FRESH FROM
THE OVEN

When the first snow envelops the countryside in
a white cloak and the garden goes into winter
hibernation, we make ourselves cosy indoors with
a warming mug of tea. To boost our spirits, nothing
can beat a sweet pastry with beetroot, cranberries,
and fine spices, still warm from the oven.

MINI FRUIT PIES

With Apple & Cranberry Filling

If we had to find another term to convey the meaning of "comfort" we would definitely opt for "pie". As the weather gets cooler, what could be better than baking these sweet and satisfying individual pies to be enjoyed with a glass of fruit punch?

☞ *MAKES 18 PIES*

SHORTCRUST PASTRY

110g (3³/₄oz) mild coconut oil

100g (3¹/₂oz) wholemeal spelt, emmer, or einkorn flour

150g (5¹/₂oz) spelt flour, plus extra for dusting

2 tsp dark muscovado sugar

pinch of salt

FILLING

165g (5³/₄oz) apples (about 2 small apples), peeled, quartered, cored, and cut into small pieces

80g (2³/₄oz) frozen cranberries, thawed

1 tbsp dark muscovado sugar

2 tsp ground cinnamon

1 tbsp lemon juice

ALSO

2 tbsp plant-based milk

1 tbsp dark muscovado sugar

Melt the coconut oil in a pan over a low heat and set aside for about 15 minutes. Combine both types of flour, the sugar, and salt in a bowl. Add the coconut oil and quickly rub the ingredients together. Avoid overhandling the pastry; it should remain fairly rough. Add 70ml (2¹/₂fl oz) water and continue to work briefly. Wrap the pastry in cling film and chill in the fridge for 20 minutes.

Meanwhile, to make the filling, bring the chopped apple, cranberries, 120ml (4fl oz) of water, and the remaining filling ingredients to the boil in a pan. Lower the heat and simmer everything for 5–7 minutes, until the cranberries have split open. Leave the filling to cool.

Preheat the oven to 180°C (350°F/Gas 4). Roll out the shortcrust on a floured work surface until 3–5mm (¹/₈–¹/₄in) thick and stamp out rounds (8cm/3 ¹/₄in in diameter). Place half of the pastry rounds on two baking trays lined with baking parchment. For the lids, use a piping bag nozzle or a thimble to stamp out 3 little circles in the remaining pastry rounds. Alternatively, make 3 little incisions in the lids using a knife. Place the filling in the centre of the pie bases, leaving a 1cm (¹/₂in) border all the way round. Place the pie lids on top, press down the edges firmly, and use a fork to seal them in place. Brush the hand pies with the milk and sprinkle with the sugar. Bake each tray in the centre of the oven for 25–30 minutes, until golden brown.

    25 MINS  *50–60 MINS* ❄ *20 MINS*

SCONES

Apple & Hazelnut – Cherry & Vanilla – Rose Hip

Scones are perfect whatever the occasion – not just with the traditional afternoon cream tea. They are simply unbeatable, particularly if served fresh from the oven with a cup of tea. In this recipe, we would like to introduce you to our three favourite and rather unusual versions.

☞ *MAKES 8 SCONES*

VERSION 1

50g (1³/₄oz) hazelnuts

100g (3¹/₂oz) apples (about
  ½ apple), peeled, cored,
  and finely diced

½ tsp ground cinnamon

VERSION 2

75g (2¹/₂oz) dried sour cherries

3¹/₂ tbsp apple juice

2–3 drops vanilla extract

VERSION 3

30g (1oz) dried rose hips,
  chopped

3¹/₂ tbsp orange juice

BASIC SCONE MIX

200g (7oz) spelt flour, plus
  extra for dusting

2 tsp baking powder

3 tsp dark muscovado sugar

pinch of salt

60g (2oz) chilled butter

140g (5oz) buttermilk

some milk for brushing

honey, clotted cream, butter,
  and jam, to serve

VERSION 1   Toast the hazelnuts in a dry pan, leave to cool then chop. Combine the hazelnuts, diced apple, and cinnamon.

VERSION 2   Soak the sour cherries in the apple juice for 1 hour. Pour away the juice, leave to drain well, then add the vanilla extract.

VERSION 3   Soak the rose hips for 1 hour in the orange juice. Pour off the juice and leave to drain well.

BASIC SCONE MIX   Preheat the oven to 220°C (425°F/Gas 7). Combine the flour, baking powder, sugar, and salt in a bowl. Add the butter in little blobs and rub everything together by hand to form crumbs. Add the buttermilk and work it in swiftly. Fold your chosen pre-prepared fruit or nut and fruit combination into the basic scone mix.

Roll out the scone dough on a floured work surface until it is roughly 2–3cm (³/₄–1¹/₂in) thick. Stamp out circles (6cm/2¹/₂in in diameter) and place upside down on a baking tray lined with baking parchment. Brush with milk and bake in the centre of the oven for 9–12 minutes, until the scones have risen nicely and are golden brown. Serve while still warm. These go wonderfully with honey or clotted cream, butter, and jam.

 | *10 MINS*    *9–12 MINS*   *IF APPLICABLE, 1 HR*

BEETROOT BUNDT CAKE

Poppy Seeds, Vanilla & Pear

The inspiration for this fantastic recipe came from some freshly squeezed juice made using beetroot, pears, and celery. The earthy tones of the beetroot mingle with the fruity pear and the poppy seeds to give this charming food pairing a wonderful nuttiness. The whole ensemble is just as convincing in bundt cake form!

☞ *MAKES 1 BUNDT CAKE (DIAMETER 22CM/8½IN)*

CAKE MIXTURE

5 eggs

150ml (5fl oz) maple syrup

250ml (9fl oz) mild vegetable oil, plus extra for greasing

2–3 drops vanilla extract

200g (7oz) almond flour, plus extra for dusting

175g (6oz) cornflour

25g (scant 1oz) poppy seeds

5 tsp baking powder

pinch of salt

250ml (9fl oz) almond milk

2 tbsp rum

80g (2¾oz) beetroot

½ pear, about 80g/2¾oz, peeled, cored, and cut into small pieces

ICING

1 quantity cashew icing (see page 193)

2 tsp beetroot powder

ALSO

½ tsp poppy seeds, to decorate

Preheat the oven to 180°C (350°F/Gas 4). Beat the eggs and maple syrup in a bowl for several minutes with an electric whisk, gradually adding the oil and vanilla extract. In a second bowl, combine the almond flour, cornflour, poppy seeds, baking powder, and salt. Add this in batches to the egg mixture, alternating with the almond milk and rum and mixing everything gently.

Place the beetroots in a pan of water and bring to the boil. Lower the heat and simmer for 45–60 minutes, until soft. Drain, submerge in cold water, peel, leave to cool, and grate coarsely or finely dice. Carefully fold the beetroot and pear into the cake mix.

Grease a bundt tin (diameter 22cm/8½in) with oil and dust with the flour. Transfer the cake mix into the tin and bake in the centre of the oven for about 1 hour, until the cake has risen and is golden brown When an inserted wooden skewer comes out clean, the bundt cake is ready. Leave to cool in the tin for about 10 minutes, then turn out onto a wire rack and leave to cool completely.

Colour the cashew icing with beetroot powder and use to decorate the cake. Scatter over the poppy seeds.

   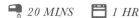 *20 MINS*   *1 HR*

FIG AND WALNUT BARS
Fig Filling & Nutty Crust

When everyday stress is getting you down, what you need is a quick snack. To make sure you really do get an energy boost, we have created this healthier muesli bar with three layers: base, fruit filling, and crunchy nut topping. It's the ideal power snack to keep you going!

☞ *MAKES 12 BARS*

BASE

15g (½oz) linseed

100g (3½oz) walnuts

40g (1¼oz) hazelnuts

200g (7oz) jumbo oats
   (gluten-free)

60g (2oz) apple purée
   (see page 192)

2 tbsp maple syrup

1 tbsp mild coconut oil, plus
   extra for greasing

2–3 drops vanilla extract

½ tsp baking powder

pinch of salt

FILLING

300g (10oz) dried figs, roughly
   chopped

2–3 drops vanilla extract

125g (4½oz) apple purée
   (see page 192)

grated zest of 1 organic orange

100g (3½oz) walnuts, roughly
   chopped

40g (1¼oz) hazelnuts, roughly
   chopped

Grind the linseed for the base using a pestle and mortar. Combine with 3½ tablespoons of water in a small bowl and leave to swell for 15 minutes, until the mixture has a gel-like consistency.

Meanwhile, preheat the oven to 180°C (350°F/Gas 4). Lightly toast the walnuts and hazelnuts in a dry pan until pale brown. Leave the nuts to cool completely. Grind 100g (3½oz) of the oats in a food processor to make a coarse flour. Add the toasted walnuts and hazelnuts and blitz briefly until the mixture has been ground to a sandy texture. Add the linseed gel, apple purée, maple syrup, coconut oil, and vanilla extract and pulse briefly in the food processor until the mixture has come together. Transfer into a large bowl and combine by hand with the remaining oats, baking powder, and salt. Grease a square baking tin (20 x 20cm/8 x 8in) with coconut oil. Put two-thirds of the mixture into the tin and press down firmly with damp hands.

To make the filling, put the figs in the food processor. Add the vanilla extract, apple purée, and orange zest and process until you have a fine paste. Spread this fig paste over the mixture and smooth the surface. Cover the filling with the remaining base mixture. Scatter the walnuts and hazelnuts over, making sure they are evenly distributed and covering the whole surface, then press gently into the fig mixture. Bake in the centre of the oven for 25–30 minutes, until the top is a pale golden-brown colour. Leave to cool completely before cutting into 12 bars. If stored in an airtight container and refrigerated, the fig and walnut bars will keep for up to 5 days.

     *25 MINS*   *25–30 MINS*

BUILDING BLOCKS: BANANA BREAD

One Loaf – Lots of Options

 FOR 1 LOAF (LOAF TIN 11 × 25CM/4½ X 10IN)

① THE BASIC INGREDIENTS

2 tbsp linseed, crushed
180g jumbo oats (gluten-free)
150g (5½oz) spelt flour, plus extra for dusting
2 tsp baking powder
pinch of salt
120g (4¼oz) dried dates, finely chopped
150ml (5fl oz) almond milk
2–3 drops vanilla extract
1 tbsp cider vinegar
3 large bananas, peeled and mashed
+ 1 banana for decoration
vegetable oil, for greasing

Preheat the oven to 180°C (350°F/Gas 4). Stir the linseed into 6 tablespoons of water and leave to swell for 15 minutes, until the mixture has a gel-like consistency. Grind the oats in a food processor to make flour. Combine the ground oats, spelt flour, baking powder, and salt in a bowl. Blitz the dates, almond milk, vanilla extract, and cider vinegar in a food processor until you have a fine mixture. Stir in the mashed bananas and linseed gel. Add this mixture to the dry ingredients and mix well.

② SOME CRUNCH

60g (2oz) walnuts, chopped
or
60g (2oz) almonds, chopped
or
60g (2oz) hazelnuts, chopped
or
60g (2oz) cashew nuts, chopped
or
60g (2oz) Brazil nuts, chopped
or
60g (2oz) peanuts, chopped

Optionally add your chosen chopped nuts to the mixture.

③ ADDED FLAVOUR

75g (2½oz) carrot, grated
or
75g (2½oz) courgette, grated
or
75g (2½oz) apple, grated
or
75g (2½oz) dark chocolate (70 per cent cocoa content)
or
75g (2½oz) blackberries
or
75g (2½oz) strawberries

Add your flavouring of choice and mix well.

   | *20 MINS* *60–70 MINS*

④

PREPARATION & BAKING

Grease a loaf tin (11 × 25cm/4$^{1}/_{2}$ x 10in) and dust with
the flour. Transfer the mixture to the tin and smooth the
surface. Peel the banana, slice in half lengthways, and
place both halves, cut surface facing upwards, on top of
the loaf. Bake the bread in the centre of the oven for
60–70 minutes, until risen and golden. When an
inserted wooden skewer comes out clean, the
loaf is cooked. Leave to cool in the tin
for 10 minutes, then turn it
out and leave to cool
completely.

BROWNIES

Kidney Beans, Maple Syrup & Vanilla

It might be unusual to bake brownies using kidney beans, but not only are beans "low carb" and very rich in protein, they also make the brownies super moist. And the flavour of the beans doesn't stand out — instead you get the usual delicious chocolate taste!

☞ *MAKES 16 BROWNIES*

THE BROWNIE MIX

500g (1lb 2oz) kidney beans (drained weight)

85g (3oz) mild coconut oil, plus extra for greasing

50g (1³/₄oz) jumbo oats (gluten-free)

30g (1oz) cocoa powder, plus extra for dusting

50g (1³/₄oz) nut butter (cashew or almond)

150ml (5fl oz) maple syrup

3½ tbsp almond milk

2–3 drops vanilla extract

1 tsp baking powder

pinch of salt

75g (3½oz) dark chocolate, 70 per cent cocoa content, chopped

Preheat the oven to 185°C (365°F/Gas 4¹/₂). Drain the beans well and rinse in cold water. Use a food processor to purée all the ingredients, except the chocolate, until smooth. Then fold 50g (1³/₄oz) of the chocolate into the brownie mix. Grease a square baking tin (20 x 20cm/8 x 8in) with coconut oil and dust with cocoa powder. Transfer the brownie mixture into the tin, smooth the surface, scatter over the remaining chocolate chunks, and bake for 35–40 minutes in the centre of the oven. Leave the brownie to cool in the tin, then slice into 16 squares.

Tip   *To make a vegan version you could use vegan dark chocolate.*

        *10 MINS*   *35–40 MINS*

SQUASH MUFFINS

Walnuts & Olive Oil

We love pumpkin and squash recipes. This autumnal vegetable is healthy and unbelievably tasty – what's more, it is really versatile, low in calories, and packed with vitamins. The delicate pumpkin flesh makes these muffins beautifully moist as well as providing plenty of dietary fibre and natural sweetness.

☞ *MAKES 18 MUFFINS*

MUFFIN MIXTURE

250g (9oz) pumpkin or squash
  flesh (such as Hokkaido,
  butternut), peel left on, diced

2 eggs

130g (4³/₄oz) dark
  muscovado sugar

75ml (2¹/₂fl oz) mild olive oil

75ml (2¹/₂fl oz) milk of choice
  – we use almond milk

2 cloves

120g (4¹/₄oz) wholemeal
  spelt flour

130g (4³/₄oz) spelt flour

2 tsp ground cinnamon

2 tsp baking powder

pinch of salt

60g (2oz) walnuts, roughly
  chopped

DECORATION

1 quantity cashew icing
  (see page 193)

2 tsp fruit powder

edible flowers, such as rose,
  cornflowers, lavender
  (optional)

Cook the squash in a pan with 150ml (5fl oz) water for 15 minutes, until soft. Drain thoroughly and purée in a high-sided beaker (it should produce about 200g/7oz) and leave to cool.

Preheat the oven to 180°C (350°F/Gas 4). Beat the eggs and sugar in a bowl for several minutes with an electric whisk, until the mixture is a pale cream colour. Add the oil and milk and stir in the puréed squash. Grind the cloves using a pestle and mortar. In a second bowl, combine both types of flour with the cinnamon, baking powder, and salt and add in batches to the egg mixture.

Fold the walnuts into the mixture. Fill the moulds of a muffin tray with 12 paper cases, divide the mixture evenly between the cases, and bake the muffins in the centre of the oven for 20–22 minutes, until risen and golden brown. When an inserted wooden skewer comes out clean, the muffins are ready. Remove from the tray and leave to cool on a wire rack.

To decorate, colour the cashew icing with the fruit powder. Ice the muffins and, if you wish, scatter with edible flowers.

Ⓘ | 🖮 *20 MINS* 🍳 *20–22 MINS*

BEETROOT CAKE

Dark Chocolate & Chocolate Ganache

Outstanding baking results can also be achieved with root vegetables such as beetroot. This healthy tuber ensures everything stays beautifully moist and produces a superb deep red colour. When combined with chocolate the end result is a truly sumptuous culinary delight. The highlight is the ganache!

☞ **MAKES 1 CAKE (DIAMETER 20CM/8IN)**

CAKE MIXTURE
450g (1lb) beetroot

3 eggs

pinch of salt

100g (3¹/₂oz) dark muscovado sugar

150ml (5fl oz) mild vegetable oil, plus extra for greasing

2–3 drops vanilla extract

125g (4¹/₂oz) wholemeal spelt flour, plus extra for dusting

25g (scant 1oz) cocoa powder

1 tsp baking powder

75g (2¹/₂oz) dark chocolate, 70 per cent cocoa content

GANACHE
30g (1oz) mild coconut oil

20g (³/₄oz) cocoa powder

1–2 drops vanilla extract

2 tbsp maple syrup

DECORATION
2 tsp beetroot powder

30g (1oz) dark chocolate, 70 per cent cocoa content, roughly chopped

Place the beetroots in a pan of water and bring to the boil. Lower the heat and simmer for 45–60 minutes, until soft. Drain, submerge in cold water, peel, leave to cool, and grate coarsely.

Preheat the oven to 180°C (350°F/Gas 4). Separate the eggs. Beat the egg whites and salt in a bowl with an electric whisk until stiff. In a second bowl, whisk the egg yolks and sugar, gradually adding the oil and vanilla extract. Combine the flour, cocoa powder, and baking powder. Add this to the eggs and mix briefly. Chop the chocolate and melt over a bain-marie. Fold the chocolate and beetroot into the cake mix. Finally, gently fold in the egg whites with a balloon whisk.

Grease a springform tin (diameter 20cm/8in) with oil and dust with the flour. Transfer the mixture to your tin and bake the cake in the centre of the oven for 45 minutes, until risen. When an inserted wooden skewer comes out clean, the cake is ready. Leave to cool on a wire rack.

To make the ganache, melt the ingredients over a bain-marie, stir well, and spread evenly over the cake. Chill the cake in the fridge for 30 minutes, until the ganache has set. Dust the cake with beetroot powder and scatter over the chocolate chunks.

Tip   *To make a lactose-free version, you can use vegan dark chocolate.*

    🥄 *25 MINS*   🍴 *45–60 MINS + 45 MINS*   ❄ *30 MINS*

"ELISENLEBKUCHEN"

Almonds & Lebkuchen Spices

The story behind the traditional German biscuit known as Elisenlebkuchen begins in Nuremberg, Germany, in 1395 when a baker named his "lebkuchen" biscuit recipe after his daughter Elisabeth. Ever since, in Germany these lebkuchen have been associated with the build-up to Christmas, just like mulled wine and minced pies. This recipe is particularly delicious and moist thanks to the nuts and maple syrup.

☞ *MAKES 30*
  LEBKUCHEN

THE DOUGH

2 eggs

150ml (5fl oz) maple syrup

½ tsp black cardamom seeds

6 cloves

2 whole allspice berries

3 tsp ground cinnamon

pinch of grated nutmeg

1g fresh ginger, peeled and
  finely grated

grated zest of ½ organic
  orange

pinch of salt

200g (7oz) ground almonds

100g (3½oz) wholemeal
  spelt flour or wholemeal
  einkorn flour

½ tsp baking powder

ALSO

30 edible rice paper discs
  (diameter 5cm/2in)

Beat the eggs and maple syrup in a large bowl for several minutes with an electric whisk until foamy. Finely grind the cardamom, cloves, and allspice using a pestle and mortar. In a second bowl, combine the spices, ginger, orange zest, salt, almonds, flour, and baking powder. Add the dry ingredients in batches to the egg mixture and combine to make a smooth dough.

Place the rice paper discs on three trays lined with baking parchment. Put a blob of the dough on each disc and use a moistened knife to spread the mixture into a slightly domed shape. Leave to rest for 1 hour. Preheat the oven to 180°C (350°F/Gas 4). Bake each tray in the centre of the oven for about 20 minutes, then remove and leave to cool on a wire rack.

Tip *If stored in an airtight container in a cool place, these will keep for 3–4 weeks.*

🕐 | 🔨 *15 MINS* 📟 *1 HR* 💤 *1 HR*

COURONNE

Sumptuous Yeast Garland with a Date & Nut Filling

The couronne is a variant on the galette des rois that originates in the South of France. It is a filled yeast garland, which also makes an ideal gift. We complement the yeasted spelt dough with a filling made from bitter walnuts and dried sour cherries with added dates for a natural sweetness.

☞ *MAKES 1 COURONNE*

YEAST DOUGH

½ tsp black cardamom seeds

130ml (4½fl oz) milk of choice
 – we use almond milk

20g (³/₁oz) acacia honey

5g dried yeast

pinch of salt

200g (7oz) spelt flour, plus extra
 for dusting

20g (³/₄oz) softened butter

FILLING

100g (3½oz) dried dates,
 finely chopped

70g (2¼oz) walnuts

½ tsp black cardamom seeds

1 tsp ground cinnamon

2–3 drops vanilla extract

70g (2¼oz) softened butter

30g (1oz) dried sour cherries

ALSO

1 tbsp milk of choice

1 egg yolk

Finely grind the cardamom seeds using a pestle and mortar. To make the yeast dough, heat the milk in a pan until lukewarm. Add the cardamom, honey, yeast, and salt and stir well until the yeast has completely dissolved. Use the dough hook on an electric mixer to combine the flour, yeast mixture, and butter in a bowl for a couple of minutes, until you have a glossy, supple dough. The dough may seem to be relatively soft, but this consistency is absolutely right. Cover with a tea towel and leave to prove in a warm place for 1 hour, until doubled in volume.

Meanwhile, for the filling, place the dates in a pan with 100ml (3½fl oz) water, bring them to the boil, then simmer gently until soft. Drain and leave to cool. Toast the walnuts in a dry pan and likewise leave to cool. Finely grind the cardamom seeds using a pestle and mortar. Blitz the dates, walnuts, and all the spices in a food processor or using a hand-held blender until you have a smooth paste. Add the butter and vanilla extract.

Knead the dough once again on a floured work surface and roll it out into a rectangle (about 50 × 25cm/20 x 10in). Spread the nut paste evenly over the surface. Scatter the sour cherries over the paste. Roll up the rectangle from the long side and cut it in half lengthways with a sharp knife. Arrange the halves with the filling facing upwards, join them together at one end, then twist together to create a braid. Join the two ends and lay the garland on a tray lined with baking parchment. Cover with a tea towel and leave to prove in a warm place for a further 30 minutes to 1 hour, until it has significantly increased in volume.

Preheat the oven to 180°C (350°F/Gas 4). Whisk the milk and egg yolk and brush the mixture over the garland. Bake in the centre of the oven for 10–15 minutes, until the couronne has risen and is golden.

 🥄 *20 MINS* 🍞 *10–15 MINS* 💤 *90 MINS TO 2 HRS*

PANETTONE
Hazelnuts & Dried Fruit

Panettone, a speciality from Milan, is traditionally baked at Christmas. We always feel the classic recipe is rather dry, so in our mini version we soak the dried fruit beforehand to make them more moist. Hazelnuts and almonds ensure that essential crunch.

 MAKES 12 MINI PANETTONE

YEAST DOUGH

100g (3½oz) mixed dried fruit, such as figs, dates, sour cherries, raisins, and cranberries

3½ tbsp rum

3½ tbsp orange juice

100ml (3½fl oz) milk of choice – we use almond milk

50g (1¾oz) dark muscovado sugar

2–3 drops vanilla extract

pinch of dried yeast

pinch of salt

280g (9½oz) spelt flour, plus extra for dusting

100g (3½oz) softened butter

2 eggs

grated zest of 1 organic orange and 1 organic lemon

50g (1¾oz) hazelnuts, roughly chopped

ALSO

1 tbsp milk of choice

1 egg yolk

2 tbsp flaked almonds

Ideally the night before or a couple of hours in advance, roughly chop the dried fruit, transfer to a bowl, and pour over the rum and orange juice. Leave the mixture to soak for as long as possible.

To make the yeast dough, heat the milk in a pan until lukewarm. Add the sugar, vanilla extract, yeast, and salt and stir well until the yeast has dissolved. Use the dough hook on an electric mixer to combine the flour, yeast mixture, butter, eggs, and citrus fruit zest in a bowl for a couple of minutes, until you have a glossy, supple dough. The dough will appear very soft, but this is exactly the right consistency to ensure the panettone turn out beautifully moist. Cover with a tea towel and leave to prove in a warm place for 1 hour to 1 hour 30 minutes, until doubled in volume.

Fill the moulds of a muffin tray with 12 paper cases. Drain the fruit. Work the hazelnuts and fruit into the dough. Working on a floured work surface, divide the dough into 12 portions using well-floured hands, shape each portion into a ball, and put each one into a muffin tray mould. Cover with a tea towel and leave to prove in a warm place for a further 20 minutes.

Preheat the oven to 180°C (350°F/Gas 4). Whisk the milk and egg yolk and brush over the panettone, then sprinkle with the flaked almonds. Bake in the centre of the oven for 15–20 minutes, until golden brown. The panettone taste best if eaten slightly warm.

Tip   *If you unexpectedly end up with some panettone left over, you can use it to make delicious French toast!*

 15 MINS   *15–20 MINS*   *4–12 HRS + 110 MINS*

SPICED HONEY "LEBKUCHEN"

Almonds & Orange Zest

This is a favourite advent recipe in Germany and here we bake it with wholesome spelt flour and almonds. The most important thing in terms of the flavour is to use plenty of freshly ground spices, orange zest, and honey. Instead of icing the biscuits, we decorate them with almonds, pumpkin seeds, and cranberries.

☞ *MAKES ABOUT 40 LEBKUCHEN*

THE DOUGH

4 black peppercorns

4 whole allspice berries

6 cloves

½ tsp black cardamom seeds

pinch of grated nutmeg

1 tsp ground cinnamon

½ tsp ground ginger

300g (10oz) honey

grated zest of 1 organic orange

500g (1lb 2oz) wholemeal spelt flour, plus extra for dusting

100g (3½oz) ground almonds

50g (1¾oz) almonds, chopped

5 tsp baking powder

pinch of salt

2 eggs

DECORATION

some egg white

blanched almonds, pumpkin seeds, dried cranberries (as desired)

Finely grind the pepper, allspice, cloves, and cardamom using a pestle and mortar, then combine with the other spices. Briefly heat the honey, spices, and orange zest in a pan over a low heat, stir, and set aside to cool.

Combine the flour, ground and chopped almonds, baking powder, and salt in a bowl. Add the honey mixture and the eggs, and process the ingredients for a couple of minutes using the dough hook attachment on an electric mixer to create a dough. Shape it into a ball, wrap in cling film, and leave to rest for 30 minutes in the fridge.

Preheat the oven to 180°C (350°F/Gas 4). Roll out the dough on a floured work surface until approximately 5mm (2in) thick and stamp out different shapes as desired. Place the lebkuchen spaced slightly apart on two baking trays lined with baking parchment. Brush with egg white and decorate with your choice of almonds, pumpkin seeds, and cranberries. Bake each tray in the centre of the oven for about 10 minutes, until the edges are pale brown, then remove and leave to cool on a wire rack.

Tip *If stored in an airtight container in a cool place, the lebkuchen will keep for 4–5 weeks.*

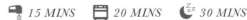 15 MINS   20 MINS   30 MINS

CRANBERRY CAKE

Almond-Coconut Sponge & Coffee-Orange Cream

☞ *MAKES 1 CAKE (DIAMETER 20CM / 8IN)*

JAM

100g (3¹/₂oz) frozen and thawed cranberries

1¹/₂ tbsp maple syrup

CAKE MIX

4 eggs

85g (3oz) dark muscovado sugar

100ml (3¹/₂fl oz) mild vegetable oil, plus extra for greasing

grated zest of 1 organic orange

150g (5¹/₂oz) almond flour, plus extra for dusting

30g (1oz) desiccated coconut

75g (2¹/₂oz) cornflour

3 tsp baking powder

pinch of salt

150ml (5fl oz) almond milk

CREAM FILLING

1 tsp coffee beans

280g (9¹/₂oz) full-fat cream cheese

125g (4¹/₂oz) almond butter

2¹/₂ tbsp maple syrup

2–3 drops vanilla extract

DECORATION

1 tbsp desiccated coconut

pink peppercorns, carnations, eucalyptus (optional)

Bring the cranberries to the boil in a pan with the maple syrup and 100ml (3¹/₂fl oz) of water. When the berries burst open, lower the heat and simmer for 5 minutes. Remove the jam from the hob and leave to cool. The jam will thicken considerably thanks to the natural pectin contained in the cranberries.

Preheat the oven to 180°C (350°F/Gas 4). Beat the eggs and sugar for several minutes in a bowl using an electric whisk. Gradually add the oil then stir in half the orange zest. In a second bowl, combine the almond flour, desiccated coconut, cornflour, baking powder, and salt and add this in batches to the egg mixture, alternating with the almond milk and stirring gently. Grease two springform tins (diameter 20cm/8in) with oil and dust with almond flour. Divide the cake mixture equally between the tins, smooth the surface, and bake in the centre of the oven for 20–25 minutes, until risen and golden brown. When an inserted wooden skewer comes out clean, the cakes are ready. Leave to cool on a wire rack.

To make the cream filling, finely grind the coffee beans using a pestle and mortar. Combine the ground coffee with the remaining ingredients and the rest of the orange zest by mixing briefly with an electric whisk.

Place one of the cakes on a cake platter and spread with the jam. Transfer the cream into a piping bag with a large round nozzle and pipe dollops of the jam on top. Place the second cake on top. Sprinkle desiccated coconut over the cake and, if you wish, decorate with pink peppercorns, carnations, and eucalyptus. Chill the cake for at least 30 minutes in the fridge before serving.

🌀 | 🍳 *30 MINS*   🍳 *20–25 MINS*   ❄ *30 MINS*

ALL ABOUT BAKING

An A to Z of ingredients – on the following pages
you will find valuable tips about baking and different
ingredients. When is each fruit or vegetable in
season? Where can I track down einkorn or teff
flour? And which foods are particularly
recommended?

FRUIT	MARCH	APRIL	MAY	JUNE	JULY	AUG
Apples						
Apricots						
Pears						
Blackberries						
Cranberries						
Strawberries						
Figs						
Blueberries						
Raspberries, red						
Raspberries, yellow						
Elderberries						
Redcurrants						
Blackcurrants						
White currants						
Mirabelle plums						
Nectarines						
Peaches						
Plums						
Plums, yellow						
Lingonberries						
Quinces						
Greengages						
Sour cherries						
Gooseberries						
Sweet cherries						
Wild strawberries						
Wild blueberries						
Grapes						
Damsons						

VEGETABLES	MARCH	APRIL	MAY	JUNE	JULY	AUG
Butternut squash						
Hokkaido squash						
Carrots						
Parsnip						
Rhubarb						
Beetroot						
Courgette						

■ peak season for local cultivation   ■ early / late season for local cultivation   ■ stored goods locally cultivated   🌿 very early to late varieties

NATURAL COLOURINGS

From Red to Purple – Organic Fruit Powders Provide Colour.

Beetroot

Blackcurrant

Blueberry

Raspberry

Strawberry

Fruit powders are produced from freeze-dried berries or vegetables such as beetroot. After drying, these are ground without any other additives. The resulting intensely coloured powders are perfect for adding natural colour to cake mixtures and creams and are available in a wide variety of shades. Not only are these powders a healthier alternative to chemically manufactured food colourings, they also add flavour and can be used to refine the aroma of the end-product. We like using fruit powders to colour cashew icing (see page 193), which we use instead of sugar frosting. Or we dust biscuits and cakes and so on with colourful powders rather than the traditional icing sugar. Leftovers also taste great in natural yogurt or smoothies, adding extra flavour at the same time.

APPLE PURÉE

☞ *MAKES APPROX
800G (1¾LB), OR
4 JARS)*

1kg (2¼lb) apples, such as
  Braeburn (roughly 6 apples)

2–3 drops vanilla extract

pinch of ground cinnamon

Add the chopped apple to a pan with the vanilla extract, cinnamon, and 100ml (3½fl oz) water and bring to the boil. Reduce the heat, cover, and simmer the apples for about 10 minutes, until soft. Purée, decant into sterilized screw-top jars while still hot, and seal with the lids. The apple purée will keep for about 3 months if stored in a cool dark place.

10 MINS   *10 MINS*

COCONUT YOGURT

☞ *MAKES 500G (1LB
2OZ) YOGURT*

1 litre (1¾ pints) coconut milk
  (60–70 per cent coconut
  extract)

10g (¼oz) cornflour

pinch of freeze-dried yogurt
  cultures (powder)

Bring the coconut milk and cornflour to the boil in a pan, stirring constantly, and simmer for 1 minute until thickened. Then leave to cool to 38°C (100.4°F) and stir in the yogurt cultures. Decant into sterilized screw-top jars or into the containers in a yogurt maker and seal with the lids. Leave to stand for 12 hours in a warm location or in your yogurt maker. Let the yogurt rest in the fridge for at least 1 day. As the yogurt matures, it will gradually set more firmly. It will keep in a sealed container in the fridge for at least 7 days.

10 MINS   *1 DAY*   *12 HRS*

COCONUT CREAM

☞ *MAKES*
  ABOUT 320G (11OZ)

400ml can coconut milk (70 per
  cent coconut extract)
1–2 drops vanilla extract

1 day in advance, put the tinned coconut milk in the fridge to chill for 24 hours. Remove and skim off just the solid coconut fat; the coconut water can be used in other recipes, for example in smoothies. Beat the coconut fat and vanilla in a bowl for 3–5 minutes, until you have a creamy, fluffy consistency. Chill the coconut cream for 5–10 minutes before use.

🖥 *5 MINS*   ❄ *5–10 MINS*

CASHEW ICING

☞ *FOR 1 CAKE –*
  MAKES 75ML
  (2½FL OZ)

BASIC RECIPE

30g (1oz) cashew nut butter

2 tbsp almond milk
  (unsweetened)

1 tsp maple syrup

1–2 drops vanilla extract

**COLOURED
VERSIONS**

in addition to the basic recipe

1 tsp almond milk
  (unsweetened)

10g (¼oz) fruit powder

Stir all the ingredients in a small bowl until smooth; the result should be a creamy icing.

For coloured versions, add a fruit powder and, if necessary, stir an additional 1 teaspoon of almond milk into the icing.

🖥 *5 MINS*

BAKING TIPS, TINS & CONVERSION TABLE

We generally cook our recipes using the **non-fan** oven setting. The fan tends to dry cakes out too much and is particularly unsuitable for sponge recipes. If your oven is somewhat older, it would be worth acquiring a digital oven thermometer.

We use size M **organic eggs** for our cakes, but the recipes also work with size L. Butter and eggs should be kept at room temperature for perfect baking results. If you need to separate eggs, however, this is easiest if they are cold. To make sure the egg whites go really stiff when you beat them, use a ceramic or stainless steel mixing bowl and wipe both the bowl and the whisk blades with some vinegar. This removes any fat residues and ensures the whites become properly stiff.

Coconut oil that has solidified can be melted in a pan over a low heat before being added to your recipe. If your cake mix includes a flour that contains gluten, this should be mixed in only briefly. Stirring for too long will result in the mixture becoming too sticky (due to excessive gluten) and the CO_2 bubbles will be too big. The mixture won't rise properly and the end result will be heavy.

Over time we have gradually acquired durable, carbon steel **baking tins**, such as Le Creuset, and cast aluminium bakeware with excellent heat conduction properties and a non-stick coating. The investment pays off because if you take care of the tins and wash them by hand, they will last a lifetime. We used the following tins for the recipes in this book:

- round ceramic ovenproof dish (diameter 24cm/9$^1/_2$in)
- small springform tin (diameter 20cm/8in)
- large springform tin (diameter 26cm/10$^1/_2$in)
- small bundt cake tin (diameter 14cm/5$^1/_2$in)
- large bundt cake tin (diameter 22cm/8$^1/_2$in)
- bundt cake / pudding basin (diameter 16cm/6$^1/_4$in) with internal tube
- muffin tray (with 5.5cm/2$^1/_4$in diameter moulds)
- tartlet tins (diameter 10cm/4in)
- tart tin (diameter 30cm/12in)
- enamel baking tray (33 × 41cm/12$^3/_4$ x 15$^3/_4$in)
- brownie tin (20.5 × 20.5cm/8$^1/_4$ x 8$^1/_4$in)
- loaf tin (11 × 25cm/4$^1/_2$ x 10in)

If you don't have a particular baking tin, use a recipe conversion: multiply each ingredient by the factor from this table. For eggs, round the number up and use size S. You may need to alter the cooking time, so always test the cake is done by inserting a skewer.

		☞ BAKING TIN SIZE AS PER RECIPE								
		Round tins (diameter in cm/in)								
		12/5	16/6$^1/_4$	18/7	20/8	22/8$^1/_2$	24/9$^1/_2$	26/10$^1/_2$	28/11	30/12	32/12$^1/_2$
NEW BAKING TIN SIZE	12/5	-	0.6	0.4	0.4	0.3	0.3	0.2	0.2	0.2	0.1
	16/6$^1/_4$	1,8	-	0.8	0.6	0.5	0.4	0.4	0.3	0.3	0.3
	18/7	2.3	1.3	-	0.8	0.7	0.6	0.5	0.4	0.4	0.3
	20/8	2.8	1.6	1.2	-	0.8	0.7	0.6	0.5	0.4	0.4
	22/8$^1/_2$	3.4	1.9	1.5	1.2	-	0.8	0.7	0.6	0.5	0.5
	24/9$^1/_2$	4.0	2.3	1.8	1.4	1.2	-	0.9	0.7	0.6	0.6
	26/10$^1/_2$	4.7	2.6	2.1	1.7	1.4	1.2	-	0.9	0.8	0.7
	28/11	5.4	3.1	2.4	2.0	1.6	1.4	1.2	-	0.9	0.8
	30/12	6.3	3.5	2.8	2.3	1.9	1.6	1.3	1.1	-	0.9
	32/12$^1/_2$	7.1	4.0	3.2	2.6	2.1	1.8	1.5	1.3	1.1	-

PRODUCT INFORMATION

*Here we provide an overview of the ingredients we use to
help make your baking healthier and more natural.*

Organic certification

Not all organic products are equal. For instance, according to consumer advisers, the seals of approval from some associations, such as the Soil Association or the Biodynamic Association, generally impose stricter requirements than the European certifications. This applies in particular to animal welfare and food processing. These official seals require that animals are kept in appropriate conditions and fed correctly. So cows are given only small amounts of concentrated feed and their primary fodder is grass and hay. The guidelines for additives in the fodder are also more stringent, and the animals can be treated with antibiotics only in exceptional cases. Also, there may be minimal additives when processing foods.

1. TYPES OF FLOUR & BAKING POWDER

Buckwheat flour

Like teff, buckwheat is a gluten free pseudocereal. The flour is ground from the whole grain and has a delicate nutty flavour. As well as being rich in iron, buckwheat flour contains particularly high levels of protein, vitamins E, B1, and B2, as well as potassium, calcium, and magnesium. For lighter and moister baking results, buckwheat flour should ideally be combined with cornflour, other types of flour, or ground nuts. You will find buckwheat flour in well-stocked supermarkets, organic shops, and health-food stores.

Spelt flour

Spelt is one of the oldest original types of cereal and our current wheat varieties have been developed from this grain. It is rich in vitamins and minerals and can sometimes be consumed by people with a wheat intolerance – even though spelt is a type of wheat. This grain contains gluten and plenty of healthy nutrients, including all eight essential amino acids. It has a total protein content of 11 per cent. The whole grain contains phosphorous, vitamins (especially certain B vitamins), silica, zinc, magnesium, manganese, iron, potassium, and copper. The high fibre content ensures you feel full for longer. Spelt is excellent for baking and can be used like wheat.

Spelt flour

This is the darkest of the ground spelt flour varieties. It has a hearty flavour and is good for yeasted doughs. It also contains lots of minerals, vitamins, and fibre from the outer hull of the spelt grain – and therefore contributes to a healthy diet.

Wholemeal spelt flour

Wholemeal spelt flour is ground using all parts of the cleaned grain and therefore contains even more fibre, minerals, trace elements, and vitamins than standard spelt flour. Depending on the recipe, we use wholemeal spelt flour by itself or in combination with other varieties of flour.

Einkorn flour

The ancient grain einkorn, which stems from wild wheat, has a nutty flavour and a high proportion of carotenoids, which give einkorn products a golden colour. It also contains higher than average levels of lots of minerals and proteins. Einkorn contains gluten and the flour is relatively coarse, similar to semolina in consistency, which gives cakes a beautiful crisp texture. You will find einkorn flour in well-stocked organic shops and health-food stores as well as from some online retailers.

Wholemeal emmer flour

Emmer is an almost forgotten variety of wheat that has a robust, nutty flavour. Organic farmers are now cultivating it once again for one important reason: thanks to its robust outer layer and dark colour, emmer is highly resistant to damage from pests and sunlight. It has a high proportion of proteins, carotenoids, zinc, and magnesium. You will find wholemeal emmer flour in well-stocked supermarkets, organic shops, health-food stores, and it is also available from online retailers.

Oats

Oats develop in the form of multiple branching panicles and are one of the healthiest cereals. Oats are produced from the entire grain and so contain lots of fibre, protein, antioxidants, polyphenols, unsaturated fatty acids, and minerals such as magnesium, phosphorous, and zinc along with valuable vitamins. Of all the grains, oats have the highest amount of vitamins B1 and B6 and are one of the most useful sources of iron. Oats are not related to wheat and are thus gluten free. However, it is recommended that people affected by coeliac disease should consume only oats that are clearly labelled as "gluten free". These varieties are specially cultivated, processed, and checked, so can be guaranteed to be free from gluten contamination.

Oat flour

You will find oat flour in well-stocked organic shops. Alternatively, you can easily make it yourself from oats. Simply grind the oats in a food processor to create flour.

Chickpea flour

Chickpea (or gram) flour is a gluten-free flour made from hulled, finely ground chickpeas. Its sweet and nutty flavour makes it ideal for sweet recipes as well as for making falafel and hummus. This relatively dry flour retains liquids well and ensures your cakes are beautifully moist. It scores well in terms of valuable dietary fibre and has a high protein content, the minerals iron, magnesium, and zinc, and also the vitamins folic acid, B1, and B6. You will find it in well-stocked supermarkets, Asian stores, and organic shops.

Cornmeal

Cornmeal consists of ground maize kernels. It is gluten free and has a characteristic yellow colour. It makes cakes and other baked items beautifully moist and crisp. We prefer to use cornmeal that has been farmed organically. It is available in well-stocked supermarkets and organic shops.

Cornflour

This culinary starch is derived from corn and is both gluten and lactose free. When combined with flour, cornflour gives cakes a lighter consistency. It is also used to help stabilize cream. You will find cornflour in well-stocked supermarkets and organic shops.

Almond flour

Almond flour has a delicate, nutty flavour and is produced by carefully grinding partially de-oiled almonds. This gluten-free flour is rich in protein, dietary fibre, calcium, and magnesium. It contains just 8–15 per cent oil, which is 25 per cent less than ground almonds. This makes it a very dry flour, allowing it to absorb moisture readily. As a result, it ensures your baking results are wonderfully moist. You will find almond flour in health-food shops and organic stores, and from online retailers.

Polenta

Polenta is cornmeal that has been produced using the whole maize kernel. This traditional Italian ingredient tastes fabulous in sweet recipes and pastries.

Rye flour

Rye flour contains lots of valuable components from the outer hull of the grain, which means that fibre and minerals are retained in the end product. This grain contains gluten and a high proportion of minerals, particularly potassium and phosphorous, and it supplies important amino acids. It also includes B-complex vitamins and vitamin E. Rye flour is excellent for using in both sweet and savoury baking.

Teff flour

Teff is a gluten-free pseudocereal, also known as lovegrass. The flour is always ground from the unhulled whole grain, which gives it a nutty flavour. Teff is rich in iron, magnesium, calcium, essential fatty acids, and complex carbohydrates. Teff flour is particularly good for baking because it retains moisture and helps the end result keep for longer. We recommended combining cornflour with teff flour to produce a lighter and fluffier texture. You will find teff flour in well-stocked supermarkets, organic shops, and health-food stores.

Baking powder

Organic baking powder consists of cream of tartar (potassium bitartrate), bicarbonate of soda, and cornflour and works as an excellent raising agent for baking. It is phosphate free, gluten free, and vegan.

2. SWEETENERS

Maple syrup

The trunk of the north American maple tree contains a sweet sap that can be tapped off by drilling small holes and then boiled down to create a syrup. This is a natural product with no added substances. It is graded depending on its quality. Grade A is the first sap of the harvest: the syrup is pale, clear, and has a mild flavour. Grade C flows from the tree somewhat later: the syrup is darker and has a stronger flavour. Maple syrup has a caramel flavour with a subtle sweetness. When purchasing, we recommend high-quality, organic brands, which guarantee that the contents are 100 per cent pure maple syrup.

Dates

Dried dates are a purely natural product. Medjool dates have a juicy consistency and a subtle flavour rather like honey. Deglet Nour dates are more common and easier to find. They are slightly firmer and have a more floury texture, their skin is tougher, and they are easier to process. Dates are rich in sugar and so have a high calorie content, but thanks to the fibre, potassium, calcium, magnesium, tryptophan, iron, and B vitamins they contain, they are still a good choice as a healthy snack. In cake mixtures, dried fruits can be used as a natural sugar substitute.

Honey, organic

Forest honey, acacia honey, rapeseed honey – this natural product is available in a range of different versions, both single origin and mixed, produced organically or conventionally. The criteria for organic honey are stringent. They range from the bee-keepers' working methods to the way in which the animals are kept. The beehives must be made exclusively from natural materials. Within three kilometres of the hives, the pastures over which the bees range must contain only wild plants or land that is being farmed organically. This same area must not contain any incineration plants or factories emitting pollutants, or any motorways. As winter fodder, the bees are to be given primarily their own honey and pollen. The wings of the queen must not be clipped. The honey must be processed carefully, avoiding any potential heat damage by ensuring that the temperature in the hive does not exceed 40°C (104°F). When harvesting the honey, it is not permitted to use chemical substances to keep the bees away. It is also prohibited to use drug treatments to combat parasites or disease. When purchasing, you should take care to note whether the honey originates locally or was produced in the UK or has been imported. We always use locally produced organic honey.

Dark muscovado sugar

Dark muscovado sugar is produced from cane sugar and contains all the minerals from the sugar cane juice. Its strong, distinctive flavour has hints of caramel or treacle. To make dark muscovado sugar the sugar cane is squeezed, filtered, then boiled down to create a syrup. This substance is ground up after cooling. No further processing takes place for the organic product. We prefer to use dark muscovado sugar from fair trade sources where farmers are paid higher prices and there is support for environmental and social projects. You will find dark muscovado sugar in well-stocked supermarkets, organic shops, and health-food stores.

3. DAIRY PRODUCE & EGGS

Eggs, organic

For our recipes we use organic eggs from free-range hens, size M (our recipes will also work with size L). It is important to us that animals are kept in good conditions and are well looked after and that sustainable methods are used on agricultural land. That's why we like to use organic eggs from laying hens where the male chicks are not gassed or culled after hatching for reasons of profit. Instead they are allowed to mature into adult chickens in good living conditions. These eggs cost a bit more in comparison with other organic eggs, which support the rearing of the male chicks.

Yogurt

As with milk, for animal welfare reasons we like to use yogurt that has been produced organically and certified by the Soil Association. Organic natural yogurt made using cow's milk, goat's milk, or sheep's milk can be found in well-stocked supermarkets and organic shops. Alternatively, you can also make our recipes using lactose-free, unsweetened yogurt made from soya, almond, or coconut.

Yogurt cultures

Yogurt cultures consist of a combination of *Lactobacilli* specifically for producing yogurt or fermented milk products. Choosing a suitable yogurt culture is crucial for the taste and texture of the end product. This will determine whether the flavour of the yogurt is mild or more traditionally acidic. A yogurt culture containing the bacteria *Streptococcus thermophilus* and *Lactobacillus bulgaricus* will produce a "classic" yogurt,

that is, set firm and with a strong flavour. For a more mellow yogurt, a culture without *Lactobacillus bulgaricus* is usually used. Probiotic yogurt can be created using *Lactobacillus acidophilus*. You will find yogurt cultures in health-food stores, pharmacies, or from online retailers such as The Kefir Company.

Coconut milk

Coconut milk is creamy, has a sweet flavour, and melts beautifully in the mouth. It is derived from the flesh of the coconut, which is finely ground with water then filtered. The coconut content in the product varies: for making yogurt you should use coconut milk with 60–70 per cent coconut content; for coconut cream use one with 70 per cent. In vegan cooking, the latter is a popular choice as a cream substitute.

Almond milk

To make gluten- and lactose-free almond milk, the almonds are first roasted then ground to a powder. This powder is then combined with water in a particular ratio and mixed thoroughly. This is followed by a resting phase, during which the mixture infuses and acquires its milky consistency before finally being strained. We prefer to use unsweetened organic almond milk with no additives, emulsifiers, or preservatives – just almonds, water, and sea salt. You will find organic almond milk in well-stocked supermarkets, health-food stores, and organic shops.

Milk, organic

Not all milk is the same. We prefer fresh, organic milk because of the emphasis on animal welfare. Farms have high standards for animal husbandry, including the quality of the pasture and animals having direct access to an exercise area, which strengthens their immune systems. Organically produced whole milk also contains more healthy omega-3 fatty acids and conjugated linoleic acid because the animals are predominantly fed on fresh grass or hay. The animals are not given any GM fodder or routine courses of antibiotics. Other milk options include organic fresh sheep's milk or goat's milk, which are mainly available from health-food shops. *See also* coconut milk, almond milk, and other plant-based milks.

Plant-based milk

Plant-based and lactose-free milk can be produced using soya, rice, oats, spelt, almonds, hazelnuts, cashews, macadamias, hemp, coconut, and lupin. For people who are allergic to nuts, the nut-free varieties should be used. Take care when purchasing to choose unsweetened products that do not contain any additives or emulsifiers. Some plant-based milks can also be made yourself (you'll find any number of useful instruction guides online).

Quark, organic

Exactly as with milk, for animal welfare reasons we like to use organic quark. Organic low-fat quark and organic full-fat quark with 20 per cent or 40 per cent fat content (made using cow's milk, goat's milk, or sheep's milk) can be obtained from well-stocked supermarkets and health-food stores.

4. BUTTER & FAT

Butter, organic

In the UK, most butter is the standard yellow "sweet cream" butter, which is either salted or unsalted. Unlike margarine, which was invented only in the 19th century, butter is a natural product with a long tradition. Organic butter is often paler than conventionally produced butter, which can be coloured using the additive beta carotene (E160a). Butter contains vitamins A, E, and K, plus iodine and selenium. Organic butter is better than conventionally produced butter in terms of the proportion of healthy fatty acids it contains (just like its source ingredient, organic milk). The proportion of lactose contained in cultured butter is also very low because it is largely eliminated thanks to the lactic acid bacteria, so people with a lactose intolerance are more likely to be able to consume this butter. If consumed in moderation, there are no health reasons to avoid using butter. At any rate, butter is preferable to margarine, which often contains hydrogenated fats, artificial additives, flavourings, soya, or palm oil, which is responsible for the destruction of rainforests.

Coconut oil

Coconut oil is produced from fully ripe coconuts using a mechanical cold pressing technique then carefully siphoned off. The end product can vary widely in quality so we like to use organically cultivated, fairtrade, virgin coconut oil with no additives. This comes from sustainable, mixed cropping systems and is produced without deforestation or creating plantations. Mild coconut oil is particularly good for baking because it doesn't have a strong flavour of its own.

Olive oil, extra virgin

Olive oil is a vegetable oil produced from the fruit and stones of the olive. The labelling system is regulated by the EU: "extra virgin olive oil" means the product is of the highest quality and has a very low acidity of less than 0.8 per cent. For baking it is best to use olive oils that have a mild flavour.

Vegetable oils

In addition to butter, we like using high-quality vegetable oils, such as rapeseed oil. This contains essential omega-3 fatty acids, which are often consumed in insufficient quantities.

5. SPICES & OTHER INGREDIENTS

Old apple varieties (see also page 124)

Polyphenols belong to the family of phytochemicals, which are beneficial to health, with some already proven effective against cancer and cardiovascular disease. Large quantities are usually contained in the peel and pips of apples. Plants require these phytochemicals for their defence systems and to protect themselves against various pests. They have a clear impact on the colour and taste of plant-based foodstuffs. Modern apple varieties have been cultivated to exclude these specific polyphenols in order to improve the aesthetics of the fruit, to prevent it from going brown rapidly after cutting, and to reduce acidity levels. This is precisely why so many of the apples currently available just taste sweet, with no acidity and minimal flavour. The proportion of polyphenols in apples is also linked to how well the fruit can be tolerated. People with an allergy to apples are more likely to be able to consume older apple varieties with higher polyphenol levels than the more modern cultivars. This is because polyphenols can deactivate apple allergens, preventing them from being absorbed by the body. In addition to this special characteristic, older apple varieties also have a higher proportion of healthy antioxidants, which are crucial for the human immune system to combat free radicals. So it's worth hunting out local farmers' markets or growers who are cultivating and selling old apple varieties such as Cox's Orange Pippin.

Flowers, edible (see also page 24)
Edible flowers are a fantastic way to decorate baked items without adding any extra calories. Before consuming, check whether the plants have been treated with chemicals. Shop-bought ornamental plants will usually have been sprayed so are best avoided. In supermarkets, seasonal edible flowers are sometimes sold in the herb section. If you want to pick flowers yourself, always do this in the open countryside or use untreated flowers from your own garden to avoid pollution. It's important to pick them at the right time because wilted flowers will not be very aromatic. The best time to pick most varieties is on a sunny morning just as the flowers have opened. Pick young flowers just before you need them as they wilt rapidly. If necessary, they can be kept fresh for a few hours in a bowl of cold water. Before use, remove the stalks and any green sepals. For many flowers, such as roses and Sweet Williams, only the petals are edible, so as far as possible the stamen should also be removed. To get rid of any dirt or concealed insects we advise carefully rinsing flowers in cold water, but don't rinse elderflowers otherwise the pollen, which is responsible for their flavour, will be washed away. In the winter months, dried flowers are ideal and can be obtained from well-stocked supermarkets, health-food shops, or from online retailers.

Cashew nut butter
Organic cashew nut butter is made from 100 per cent organic cashew kernels with no additives, emulsifiers, or stabilizers. As a result, the oil naturally contained in the product can sometimes rise to the surface, but the creamy consistency can be restored by stirring. Cashew nut butter has a delicate nutty flavour and is ideal for refining cakes and for use in vegan cooking. We use it to create our "cashew nut icing" (see page 193), which we use instead of sugar frosting.

Peanut butter
Peanut butter consists of 100 per cent ground peanuts. Different versions are available: organic, unsalted, salted, crunchy. Consumed in moderation, peanut butter is a good source of protein. It contains more unsaturated than saturated fatty acids and is also rich in fibre, potassium, antioxidants, zinc, magnesium, vitamin E, and niacin. For baking, we use smooth, unsalted, organic peanut butter that has no additives.

Fruit and vegetable powders
These powders are made from 100 per cent ripe fruit or vegetables, which have first been freeze-dried then ground without any additives. Available varieties include: blueberry, strawberry, raspberry, blackcurrant and beetroot powder. You can buy fruit powders from well-stocked health-food shops or online retailers such as Biovea.

Rose hips, dried
Rose hips are one of the fruits with the highest quantity of vitamin C. Other important nutrients they have include vitamins B1 and B2, vitamin E, provitamin A, niacin, and also flavonoids, fruit acids, and pectin. Rose hips are carefully dried whole and can be used in baking like other dried fruit. Dried rose hips with no additives can be bought online.

Ground ginger
Ground ginger is made from 100 per cent ginger root, which has been carefully dried then ground to create a powder. The powder is not quite as intense as fresh ginger, but it can add a fresh, tangy flavour to baked items. Ground ginger is ideal for baking because it is so convenient, but if you prefer to use fresh ginger, you shouldn't substitute it on a 1:1 basis because fresh ginger has a much stronger taste.

Cocoa

Cocoa powder with a high cocoa butter content ensures a better chocolate flavour. The effect of cocoa is similar to that of dark chocolate. We like to use fairtrade organic cocoa.

Cocoa nibs

Cocoa nibs are produced from cocoa beans, that is, from raw, unprocessed cocoa. The cocoa beans are hulled, broken into little pieces, then dried. Thanks to the fermentation and drying process they retain all the benefits of the raw product, such as important nutrients, and they develop a bitter flavour. Cocoa nibs are one of the original forms of cocoa and are ideal for baking. They can be found in well-stocked supermarkets, organic shops, and health-food stores.

Cardamom, green

Green cardamom is distinguished by its fresh, green pods that contain black seeds with an intense sweet and tangy flavour. Cardamom should be as fresh as possible when used because once it has been ground it rapidly loses its flavour and the active ingredients deteriorate. So only open the green pods and grind the black seeds shortly before use. Green cardamom pods can be found in well-stocked supermarkets, Asian stores, and organic shops.

Jam

Jam usually consists of minimal fruit and lots of sugar. We either create jam with less sugar ourselves for quick consumption or we look for organic jams with at least 70 per cent fruit content and which is produced using raw cane sugar or agave syrup. This kind of jam contains no refined white sugar. There are also organic jams available made from 100 per cent fruit without any additional sugar.

Bay leaves

You will find fresh bay leaves in the vegetable aisle at well-stocked supermarkets or at your health-food store. For many recipes you can use the dried variety of bay leaf instead.

Almond butter

Organic almond butter is produced from 100 per cent organic almonds and is high in protein. The colour of the product depends on whether blanched or unblanched almonds are used. Paler almond butter is purer and produced from blanched, unroasted almonds. Darker almond butter is produced from toasted, unblanched almonds and has a stronger flavour. White almond butter is less readily available and more expensive, so we tend to use the darker variety for baking.

Marzipan, organic

There are two varieties of this product available: vegan organic marzipan is produced using organic almonds and raw cane sugar. You can also buy honey marzipan, which contains organic honey in addition to almonds, but otherwise has no other additives or humectants. Organic marzipan is available from health-food shops.

Rose water

Rose water consists of an infusion of rose petals and water and it will add a floral, exotic note to your baking. Take care when purchasing that the product is genuinely rose water that has been produced for culinary purposes using unsprayed rose petals. It can be found in well-stocked supermarkets, Asian stores, health-food shops, and online.

Icing sugar

This can be used together with cornflour to help stabilize and thicken creams, fillings, and icing.

Chocolate, dark

If consumed in moderation (about 20g (^{3}/$_4$oz) per day), dark chocolate with a minimum cocoa content of 70 per cent provides a healthier alternative to milk chocolate. It causes only gradual fluctuations in blood sugar levels, which in turn prevents hunger pangs and so significantly reduces the risk of consuming unnecessary calories. This kind of chocolate also inhibits the release of stress hormones and therefore has a calming effect. The phytochemicals it contains, such as flavonoids, have a positive impact on the cardiovascular system. In addition, antioxidants protect the body's cells against free radicals and have anti-inflammatory properties. Dark chocolate can be either entirely or almost lactose free depending on its milk content. As a consequence, people with a lactose intolerance are more likely to be able to consume dark chocolate than milk chocolate. Many varieties of dark chocolate are also vegan. We prefer to use fairtrade, organic dark chocolate.

Dried fruit

When buying dried fruit, always ensure the fruit is unsulphured and unsweetened. Dried fruit is a healthier alternative to other sweet treats. It contains no fat, but has plenty of nutrients and fibre. However, due to the high sugar and calorie content, dried fruit should be enjoyed only in small quantities. One of the recommended five daily portions of fruit and vegetables may be consumed in dried form. Dried fruit also adds a natural sweetness to baked items.

Vanilla, extract

Vanilla extract comes from the vanilla pod, and is produced by infusing, or macerating, the pod in water or alcohol. Just a small amount can add a wonderfully mellow, sweet flavour to your cake, drink, or dessert. Alternatively, our recipes can always be made using the freshly scraped seeds from a vanilla pod.

Custard powder, organic

Standard custard powder contains starch, table salt, flavourings including lactose, and the colourings quinoline yellow and sunset yellow. We prefer to use organic custard powder, which, by contrast, contains only two natural ingredients: cornflour and Bourbon vanilla powder – both organically cultivated.

Cinnamon

There are two types of cinnamon: cassia and ceylon. Most cinnamon sold in the UK is cassia, with ceylon available from specialist online suppliers. We prefer to use Ceylon cinnamon, which is more refined and has a more subtle flavour than Cassia cinnamon and contains comparatively little coumarin: a flavouring

that occurs naturally in cinnamon and which should be consumed only in moderation. Organic Ceylon cinnamon is obtained exclusively from the bark of the Ceylon tree and is cultivated organically. It has a delicately spicy flavour, which also adds to the impression of sweetness in baked items.

ABOUT THE AUTHORS

Carolin Strothe is a photographer, art director, food stylist and author. She was born in the historic town of Celle, Germany. She trained for three years as a professional photographer and studied communication design in Hannover, with a particular emphasis on visual communication. In parallel to her studies, she founded her own creative studio in 2004. This enabled her to work on a freelance basis on various editorial and corporate design projects for agencies such as Scholz & Friends, and fischerAppelt. For over six years she has been developing recipes for magazines and food manufacturers. Her work as a photographer and food stylist has been published in magazines such as Better Photography, Thrive, and ORIGIN. Since 2013 she has been writing the food blog "Frau Herzblut", which was recognized at the German Food Blog Contest (1st prize, Passion & Innovation).

Her husband, **Sebastian Keitel**, is a brand strategist, user experience designer, and lecturer in Interaction Design. He was born in the Bauhaus town of Dessau. He studied information science in Salzgitter and Hannover. He has worked for creative agencies such as Publicis Pixelpark, Saatchi & Saatchi, DDB, Hirschen Group, and Heimat. In this role he has been responsible for brands from the health, leisure, tourism, and food sectors. As a strategist and designer he researches and examines different food and health trends. In a non-professional capacity he has been interested in healthy nutrition and organic farming for several years.

Carolin Strothe and Sebastian Keitel have been working collaboratively as freelancers for brands such as Die Techniker, TUI, and Alnatura for over a decade. Both authors more or less grew up in the garden. As a consequence they share a powerful love of nature and an appreciation for fine food. Both these foodies love cooking healthy recipes together using seasonal produce. They are also partial to barista-quality coffee, bicycle rides, and the culture of the swing era. They have a passion for lindy hop dancing and popping swing records on the turntable at parties.

A HUGE THANK YOU

Our heartfelt thanks go to Jamie Oliver, the "godfather" of this book, for his kind and generous support. Without him this book would never have been written. Thanks a lot, bro!

A special thank you must go to our mum and mother-in-law, Sabine Strothe, who was always on hand with help and advice, exceptional prop discoveries, and endless treasures from her garden.

For all things writing-related, sincere thanks go to the DK publishing team – Monika Schlitzer, Sarah Fischer, Natalie Knauer, Annemarie Heinel, and Caren Hummel.

We would like to thank Melanie Follmer from 3punktf (www.3punktf.de), who conjured up the most stunning hand-thrown pottery, and also Anke Treuter and Le Creuset (www.lecreuset.de) for the finest bakeware in the world. Heartfelt thanks also to Yoori Khoo, Sarah Alongi, Chris Nowak, Franziska Schlupski, Kristiane Adam, and Uwe Meilahn for our wonderful interchanges.

Particular thanks must go to our family, friends, and neighbours who repeatedly volunteered as recipe testers and gave us invaluable feedback.

Last but not least, thank you to Indigo florists for all the special requests and loans they agreed to and to the Hahne orchard for helping define the apple varieties.

For DK UK

Translator Alison Tunley
Editor Claire Cross
Senior editor Kate Meeker
Editorial assistant Poppy Blakiston Houston
Senior art editor Glenda Fisher
Jacket designer Harriet Yeomans
Producer, pre-production David Almond
Senior producer Tony Phipps
Managing editor Stephanie Farrow
Managing art editor Christine Keilty

For DK Germany

Publisher Monika Schlitzer
Managing editor Caren Hummel
Project manager Anne Heinel
Production Sabine Huttenkofer, Stefanie Staat
Production coordinator Ksenia Lebedeva
Producer Dorothee Whittaker

Recipes and text Carolin Strothe, Sebastian Keitel
Photography and styling Carolin Strothe, Sebastian Keitel
Portrait Jamie Oliver James Lyndsay

First British Edition 2019
Dorling Kindersley Limited
80 Strand, London, WC2R 0RL

A CIP catalogue record for this book
is available from the British Library.
ISBN: 978-0-2413-7771-0

Printed and bound in China

A WORLD OF IDEAS:
SEE ALL THERE IS TO KNOW

www.dk.com